Great Predictions

Data Analysis and Probability

BRITANNICA
Mathematics in Context

TEACHER'S GUIDE

HOLT, RINEHART AND WINSTON

Mathematics in Context is a comprehensive curriculum for the middle grades.
It was developed in 1991 through 1997 in collaboration with the Wisconsin Center
for Education Research, School of Education, University of Wisconsin-Madison and
the Freudenthal Institute at the University of Utrecht, The Netherlands, with the
support of the National Science Foundation Grant No. 9054928.

The revision of the curriculum was carried out in 2003 through 2005, with the
support of the National Science Foundation Grant No. ESI 0137414.

 National Science Foundation
Opinions expressed are those of the authors
and not necessarily those of the Foundation.

Roodhardt, A.; Wijers, M.; Bakker, A.; Cole, B. R.; and Burrill, G. (2006).
Great predictions. In Wisconsin Center for Education Research & Freudenthal
Institute (Eds.), *Mathematics in context.* Chicago: Encyclopædia Britannica, Inc.

The Teacher's Guide for this unit was prepared by David C. Webb, Beth R. Cole,
Monica Wijers, Truus Dekker, and Sonia Palha.

ISBN 0-03-039834-7

3 4 5 6   073   09 08 07

The *Mathematics in Context* Development Team

Development 1991–1997

The initial version of *Great Expectations* was developed by Anton Roodhardt and Monica Wijers. It was adapted for use in American schools by Beth R. Cole and Gail Burrill.

Wisconsin Center for Education Research Staff

Thomas A. Romberg
Director

Joan Daniels Pedro
Assistant to the Director

Gail Burrill
Coordinator

Margaret R. Meyer
Coordinator

Freudenthal Institute Staff

Jan de Lange
Director

Els Feijs
Coordinator

Martin van Reeuwijk
Coordinator

Project Staff

Jonathan Brendefur
Laura Brinker
James Browne
Jack Burrill
Rose Byrd
Peter Christiansen
Barbara Clarke
Doug Clarke
Beth R. Cole
Fae Dremock
Mary Ann Fix

Sherian Foster
James A, Middleton
Jasmina Milinkovic
Margaret A. Pligge
Mary C. Shafer
Julia A. Shew
Aaron N. Simon
Marvin Smith
Stephanie Z. Smith
Mary S. Spence

Mieke Abels
Nina Boswinkel
Frans van Galen
Koeno Gravemeijer
Marja van den Heuvel-Panhuizen
Jan Auke de Jong
Vincent Jonker
Ronald Keijzer
Martin Kindt

Jansie Niehaus
Nanda Querelle
Anton Roodhardt
Leen Streefland
Adri Treffers
Monica Wijers
Astrid de Wild

Revision 2003–2005

The revised version of *Great Predictions* was developed Arthur Bakker and Monica Wijers. It was adapted for use in American Schools by Gail Burrill.

Wisconsin Center for Education Research Staff

Thomas A. Romberg
Director

David C. Webb
Coordinator

Gail Burrill
Editorial Coordinator

Margaret A. Pligge
Editorial Coordinator

Freudenthal Institute Staff

Jan de Lange
Director

Truus Dekker
Coordinator

Mieke Abels
Content Coordinator

Monica Wijers
Content Coordinator

Project Staff

Sarah Ailts
Beth R. Cole
Erin Hazlett
Teri Hedges
Karen Hoiberg
Carrie Johnson
Jean Krusi
Elaine McGrath

Margaret R. Meyer
Anne Park
Bryna Rappaport
Kathleen A. Steele
Ana C. Stephens
Candace Ulmer
Jill Vettrus

Arthur Bakker
Peter Boon
Els Feijs
Dédé de Haan
Martin Kindt

Nathalie Kuijpers
Huub Nilwik
Sonia Palha
Nanda Querelle
Martin van Reeuwijk

Cover photo credits: (left, middle) © Getty Images; (right) © Comstock Images

Illustrations
xii (left) Jason Millet; **8** Holly Cooper-Olds; **12** James Alexander; **17, 18, 24** Holly Cooper-Olds; **28, 29** James Alexander; **34, 36, 40** Christine McCabe/© Encyclopædia Britannica, Inc.; **44** Holly Cooper-Olds

Photographs
xii Amos Morgan/PhotoDisc/Getty Images; **xix** PhotoDisc/Getty Images; **xx** Peter Van Steen/ HRW Photo; **1** Photodisc/Getty Images; **2** © Raymond Gehman/Corbis; **3** USDA Forest Service– Region; **4** Archives, USDA Forest Service, www.forestryimages.org; **7** © Robert Holmes/Corbis; **16** laozein/Alamy; **18** © Corbis; **30** Victoria Smith/HRW; **32** Epcot Images/Alamy; **36** Dennis MacDonald/ Alamy; **39** Creatas; **42** (left to right) © PhotoDisc/Getty Images; © Corbis; **44** Dennis MacDonald/ Alamy; **45** Dynamic Graphics Group/ Creatas/Alamy; **47** © Corbis

Contents

Dear Teacher,

Welcome! *Mathematics in Context* is designed to reflect the National Council of Teachers of Mathematics Principles and Standards for School Mathematics and the results of decades of classroom-based education research. *Mathematics in Context* was designed according to the principles of Realistic Mathematics Education, a Dutch approach to mathematics teaching and learning where mathematical content is grounded in a variety of realistic contexts in order to promote student engagement and understanding of mathematics. The term *realistic* is meant to convey that the contexts and mathematics can be made "real in your mind." Rather than relying on you to explain and demonstrate generalized definitions, rules, or algorithms, students investigate questions directly related to a particular context and develop mathematical understanding and meaning from that context.

The curriculum encompasses nine units per grade level. *Great Predictions* is designed to be the last unit in the Data Analysis and Probability strand, but it also lends itself to independent use—to introduce students to experiences that will enrich their understanding of sampling, using and finding probabilities, counting strategies, and making predictions for events. In addition to the Teacher's Guide and Student Books, *Mathematics in Context* offers the following components that will inform and support your teaching:

- *Teacher Implementation Guide,* **which provides an overview of the complete system and resources for program implementation;**

- *Number Tools* and *Algebra Tools,* **which are black-line master resources that serve as intervention sheets or practice pages to support the development of basic skills and extend student understanding of concepts developed in Number and Algebra units; and**

- *Mathematics in Context Online,* **which is a rich, balanced resource for teachers, students, and parents looking for additional information, activities, tools, and support to further students' mathematical understanding and achievements.**

Thank you for choosing *Mathematics in Context.* We wish you success and inspiration!

Sincerely,

The Mathematics in Context Development Team

Great Predictions and the NCTM Principles and Standards for School Mathematics for Grades 6–8

The process standards of Problem Solving, Reasoning and Proof, Communication, Connections, and Representation are addressed across all *Mathematics in Context* units.

In addition, this unit specifically addresses the following PSSM content standards and expectations:

Data Analysis and Probability

In grades 6–8, all students should:

- select, create, and use appropriate graphical representations of data;
- find, use, and interpret measures of center and spread;
- discuss and understand the correspondence between data sets and their graphical representations;
- use observations about differences between two or more samples to make conjectures about the populations from which the samples were taken;
- use conjectures to formulate new questions and plan new studies to answer them;
- understand and use appropriate terminology to describe complementary and mutually exclusive events;
- use proportionality and a basic understanding of probability to make and test conjectures about the results of experiments and simulations; and
- compute probabilities for simple compound events, using such methods as organized lists, tree diagrams, and area models.

In grades 9–12, all students should:

- use simulations to construct empirical probability distributions;
- compute and interpret the expected value of random variables in simple cases;
- understand the concepts of conditional probability and independent events; and
- understand how to compute the probability of a compound event.

Geometry

In grades 6–8, all students should:

- use geometric models to represent and explain numerical relationships.

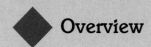
Math in the Unit

Prior Knowledge

Great Predictions is the final unit in the Data Analysis and Probability strand. It assumes students have worked through all the units in this strand and know and can do the following with understanding:

- add, subtract, multiply, and divide rational numbers in all representations;

- use fractions, decimals, and percents to solve problems, as in the Number units;

- use and find experimental and theoretical chances and express a chance as a ratio of the number of favorable outcomes to the total number of possible outcomes, as formalized in the unit *Second Chance*;

- use organized counting techniques and strategies;

- understand and use statistical measures (mean, median, mode, spread), as introduced and used in the units *Picturing Numbers, Dealing with Data,* and *Insights into Data.*

- understand, make, and interpret statistical graphs such as number line plots and histograms, as introduced in the units *Picturing Numbers* and *Dealing with Data*;

- know and understand the terms population and sample, as introduced and used in the units *Dealing with Data* and *Insights into Data*;

- recognize possible bias in samples and survey results, as introduced in the unit *Insights into Data*;

- collect and represent data through surveys, experiments, and simulations, as introduced in the units *Second Chance* and *Insights into Data*;

- use tree diagrams, as introduced in the unit *Take a Chance*, and chance trees, two-way tables, and the area model, as introduced in the unit *Second Chance*.

Great Predictions is the last unit in the Data Analysis and Probability strand and integrates concepts from both strands. The unit explores such topics as representative and biased samples, dependent and independent events, expected values, and joint probability.

Descriptions of unusual events lead to a deeper understanding of the mathematical concepts of representative, biased, and random samples. Students reason about how likely it is that certain events will occur.

They explore questions such as: *Are unusual events, those which differ from expected outcomes, due to chance, or can the results be explained by a deeper investigation? Can results from a sample be used to make reliable estimates for the population or not? And on what does this depend?* Surveys provide the context for describing an unknown population and investigating sources of bias.

By studying samples and taking samples with varying sample size, students learn in more depth that drawing conclusions from samples always involves uncertainty. Students also experience that small samples can have great variability. Recording the results of an increasing sample size for example, by combining results of samples collected by a whole class, helps students realize that variability can decrease if sample size increases and that a larger sample is more likely to be representative of the population. Students use data from various samples to estimate chances of particular events.

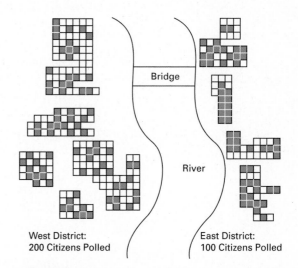

West District:
200 Citizens Polled

East District:
100 Citizens Polled

An opinion poll about building a bridge across a river formally introduces the concept of dependent and independent events. Students use tree diagrams, chance trees, and tables to organize information and make inferences about whether events seem to be dependent or not. Students are made aware of the fact that although using these models can help them decide if two events are possibly dependent, they cannot help them find out why a connection exists. Some situations from earlier units are revisited, and the dependency of events is formally addressed.

Chance trees that were introduced in the unit *Second Chance*—as a special type of tree diagram—are used to explore and calculate expected values. To make the calculation of the expected value easier to understand, now numbers are used in the chance trees, such as in the example shown.

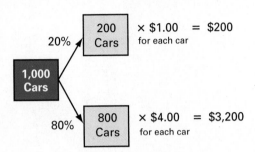

The expected toll in this example can be found by adding the total toll collected, which is $3,400, and dividing this over the 1,000 cars, which results in an expected toll of $3.40 per car. Students investigate what happens if they start with a different number of cars, which leads to the notion that the expected value only depends on the chances of the different outcomes. This notion is addressed in a preformal way.

Students continue the study of chances of combined event situations, which began in the unit *Second Chance*. They explore more complex situations using chance trees and area models. The multiplication rule for chance is formalized in this unit. Students find out that this rule will not always work, such as in the case of dependent events.

iii.

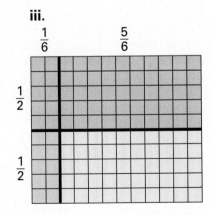

When students have finished the unit, they:

- understand the relationship between a sample and a population;
  - Samples were informally introduced in the unit *Dealing with Data*, and revisted preformally in the unit *Insight into Data*.
  - Students can draw conclusions from samples, and they know that uncertainty or chance is involved when doing this.
  - Students know that samples must be large enough and randomly chosen to give a good image of the population.
  - Students understand the concepts of randomness and bias.
- understand the difference between independent and dependent events;
  - Students use information from two-way tables or tree diagrams to decide whether events are dependent or independent.
  - Students understand that if events are dependent, this does not tell why a connection exists. This may be due to chance.
- calculate and use expected value to make decisions;
  - Students can calculate expected value from a chance tree or a table.
- understand the meaning of chance or probability and can estimate and compute chances; and
  - Students can find chances as relative frequencies from tables and graphs.
  - Students can calculate chances in multi-event situations using chance trees or an area model. These models were introduced and used in the units *Take a Chance* and *Second Chance*.
  - The multiplication rule for chances (for independent events) is formalized in this unit.
- can make connections between statistics and probability.
  - Students can use data to compute chances.

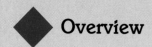

The Data Analysis and Probability Strand: An Overview

One thing is for sure: our lives are full of uncertainty. We are not certain what the weather will be tomorrow or which team will win a game or how accurate a pulse rate really is. Data analysis and probability are ways to help us measure variability and uncertainty. A central feature of both data analysis and probability is that these disciplines help us make numerical conjectures about important questions.

The techniques and tools of data analysis and probability allow us to understand general patterns for a set of outcomes from a given situation, such as tossing a coin, but it is important to remember that a given outcome is only part of the larger pattern. Many students initially tend to think of individual cases and events, but gradually they learn to think of all features of data sets and of probabilities as proportions in the long run.

The MiC Approach to Data Analysis and Probability

The Data Analysis and Probability units in MiC emphasize dealing with data, developing an understanding of chance and probability, using probability in situations connected to data analysis, and developing critical thinking skills.

 The strand begins with students' intuitive understanding of the data analysis concepts of *most*, *least*, and *middle* in relation to different types of *graphical representations* that show *the distribution of data* and the probability concepts of *fairness* and *chance*. As students gradually formalize these ideas, they use a variety of counting strategies and graphical representations. In the culminating units of this strand, they use formal rules and strategies for calculating probabilities and finding measures of central tendency and spread.

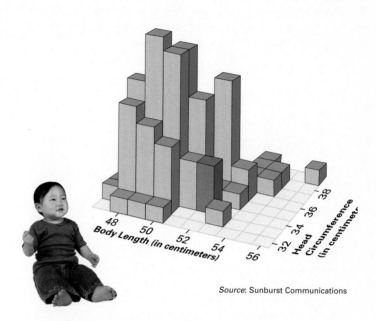

Source: Sunburst Communications

Throughout this development, there is a constant emphasis on interpreting conclusions made by students and suggested in the media or other sources. In order for students to make informed decisions, they must understand how information is collected, represented, and summarized, and they examine conjectures made from the information based on this understanding. They learn about all phases of an investigative cycle, starting with questions, collecting data, analyzing them, and communicating about the conclusions. They are introduced to inference-by-sampling to collect data and reflect on possible sources of bias. They develop notions of random sampling, variation and central tendency, correlation, and regression. Students create, interpret, and reflect on a wide range of graphical representations of data and relate these representations to numerical summaries such as mean, mode, and range.

Organization of the Strand

Statistical reasoning based on data is addressed in all Data Analysis and Probability units. Students' work in these units is organized into two substrands: Data Analysis and Chance. As illustrated in the following map of the strand, the three core units that focus on data analysis are *Picturing Numbers*, *Dealing with Data*, and *Insights into Data*. The two units that focus on probability are *Take a Chance* and *Second Chance*. The sixth core unit in this strand, *Great Predictions*, integrates data analysis and probability.

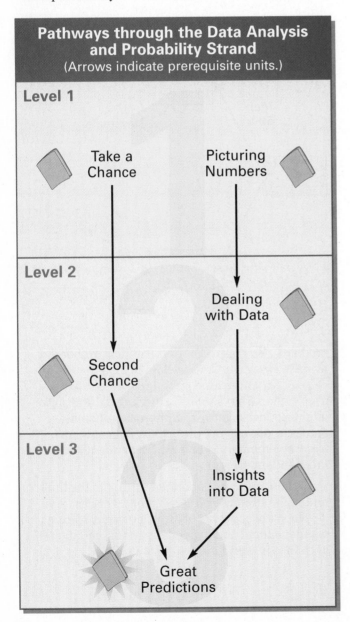

Pathways through the Data Analysis and Probability Strand
(Arrows indicate prerequisite units.)

Level 1
Take a Chance
Picturing Numbers

Level 2
Dealing with Data
Second Chance

Level 3
Insights into Data
Great Predictions

Data Analysis

In the units of the Data Analysis substrand, students collect, depict, describe, and analyze data. Using the statistical tools they develop, they make inferences and draw conclusions based on data sets.

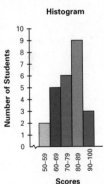

Number of Babies in Litter

The substrand begins with *Picturing Numbers*. Students collect data and display them in tabular and graphical forms, such as histograms, number line plots, and pie charts. Measures of central tendency, such as the mean, are used informally as students interpret data and make conjectures.

In *Dealing with Data*, students create and interpret scatter plots, box plots, and stem-and-leaf plots, in addition to other graphical representations. The mean, median, mode, range, and quartiles are used to summarize data sets. Students investigate data sets with outliers and make conclusions about the appropriate use of the mean and median.

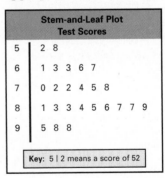

Stem-and-Leaf Plot
Test Scores

5	2 8
6	1 3 3 6 7
7	0 2 2 4 5 8
8	1 3 3 4 5 6 7 7 9
9	5 8 8

Key: 5 | 2 means a score of 52

Histogram

Sampling is addressed across this substrand, but in particular in *Insights into Data*, starting with informal notions of representative samples, randomness, and bias. Students gather data using various sampling techniques and investigate the differences between a survey and a sample. They create a simulation to answer questions about a situation. Students also consider how graphical information can be misleading, and they are introduced informally to the concepts of regression and correlation.

In *Great Predictions*, students learn to recognize the variability in random samples and deepen their understanding of the key statistical concepts of randomness, sample size, and bias. As the capstone unit to the Data Analysis and Probability strand, data and chance concepts and techniques are integrated and used to inform conclusions about data.

Chance

Beginning with the concept of fairness, *Take a Chance* progresses to everyday situations involving chance. Students use coins and number cubes to conduct repeated trials of an experiment. A chance ladder is used as a model throughout the unit to represent the range from impossible to certain and to ground the measure of chance as a number between 0 and 1. Students also use tree diagrams to organize and count, and they use benchmark fractions, ratios, and percents to describe the probability of various outcomes and combinations.

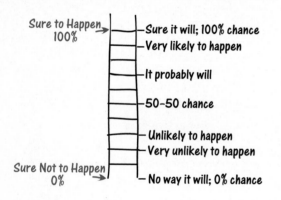

The second probability unit, *Second Chance*, further develops students' understanding of fairness and the quantification of chance. Students make chance statements from data presented in two-way tables and in graphs.

	Men	Women	Total
Glasses	32	3	35
No Glasses	56	39	95
Total	88	42	130

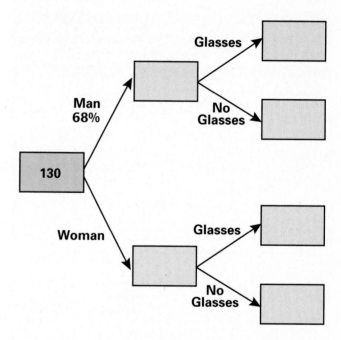

Students also reason about theoretical probability and use chance trees as well as an area model to compute chances for compound events. They use information from surveys, experiments, and simulations to investigate experimental probability. Students also explore probability concepts such as complementary events and dependent and independent events.

These concepts are elaborated further in the final unit of the strand, *Great Predictions*. This last unit develops the concepts of expected value, features of independent and dependent events, and the role of chance in world events.

Critical Reasoning

Critical reasoning about data and chance is a theme that exists in every unit of the Data Analysis and Probability strand. In *Picturing Numbers*, students informally consider factors that influence data collection, such as the wording of questions on a survey, and they compare different graphs of the same data set. They also use statistical data to build arguments for or against environmental policies.

In *Take a Chance*, students use their informal knowledge of fairness and equal chances as they evaluate decision-making strategies.

In *Dealing with Data*, students explore how the graphical representation of a data set influences the conjectures and conclusions that are suggested by the data. They compare advantages and disadvantages of various graphs and explore what you learn from using different measures of central tendency.

Throughout the curriculum, students are asked to view representations critically. Developing a critical attitude is especially promoted in *Insights into Data*, when students analyze graphs from mass media.

In *Second Chance*, students explore the notion of dependency (for instance, the relation of gender and wearing glasses) and analyze statements about probabilities (for instance, about guessing during a test).

In *Great Predictions*, students study unusual samples to decide whether they occurred by chance or for some other reason (pollution, for instance). They explore how expected values and probability can help them make decisions and when this information could be misleading.

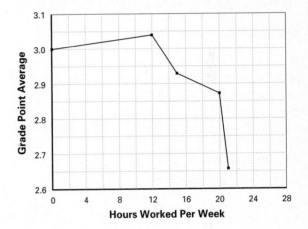

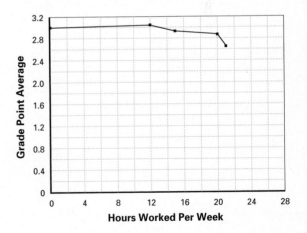

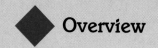

Student Assessment in Mathematics in Context

As recommended by the NCTM *Principles and Standards for School Mathematics* and research on student learning, classroom assessment should be based on evidence drawn from several sources. An assessment plan for a *Mathematics in Context* unit may draw from the following overlapping sources:

- **observation—As students work individually or in groups, watch for evidence of their understanding of the mathematics.**
- **interactive responses—Listen closely to how students respond to your questions and to the responses of other students.**
- **products—Look for clarity and quality of thought in students' solutions to problems completed in class, homework, extensions, projects, quizzes, and tests.**

Assessment Pyramid

When designing a comprehensive assessment program, the assessment tasks used should be distributed across the following three dimensions: mathematics content, levels of reasoning, and difficulty level. The Assessment Pyramid, based on Jan de Lange's theory of assessment, is a model used to suggest how items should be distributed across these three dimensions. Over time, assessment questions should "fill" the pyramid.

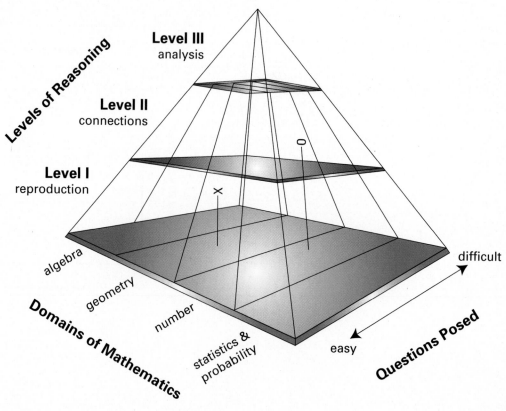

Levels of Reasoning

Level I questions typically address:

- recall of facts and definitions and
- use of technical skills, tools, and standard algorithms.

As shown in the pyramid, Level I questions are not necessarily easy. For example, Level I questions may involve complicated computation problems. In general, Level I questions assess basic knowledge and procedures that may have been emphasized during instruction. The format for this type of question is usually short answer, fill-in, or multiple choice. On a quiz or test, Level I questions closely resemble questions that are regularly found in a given unit, substituted with different numbers and/or contexts.

Level II questions require students to:

- integrate information;
- decide which mathematical models or tools to use for a given situation; and
- solve unfamiliar problems in a context, based on the mathematical content of the unit.

Level II questions are typically written to elicit short or extended responses. Students choose their own strategies, use a variety of mathematical models, and explain how they solved a problem.

Level III questions require students to:

- make their own assumptions to solve open-ended problems;
- analyze, interpret, synthesize, reflect; and
- develop one's own strategies or mathematical models.

Level III questions are always open-ended problems. Often, more than one answer is possible and there is a wide variation in reasoning and explanations. There are limitations to the type of Level III problems that students can be reasonably expected to respond to on time-restricted tests.

The instructional decisions a teacher makes as he or she progresses through a unit may influence the level of reasoning required to solve problems. If a method of problem solving required to solve a Level III problem is repeatedly emphasized during instruction, the level of reasoning required to solve a Level II or III problem may be reduced to recall knowledge, or Level I reasoning. A student who does not master a specific algorithm during a unit but solves a problem correctly using his or her own invented strategy may demonstrate higher-level reasoning than a student who memorizes and applies an algorithm.

The "volume" represented by each level of the Assessment Pyramid serves as a guideline for the distribution of problems and use of score points over the three reasoning levels.

These assessment design principles are used throughout *Mathematics in Context*. The Goals and Assessment charts that highlight ongoing assessment opportunities—on pages xvi and xvii of each Teacher's Guide—are organized according to levels of reasoning.

In the Lesson Notes section of the Teacher's Guide, ongoing assessment opportunities are also shown in the Assessment Pyramid icon located at the bottom of the Notes column.

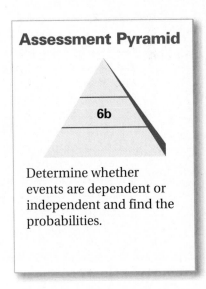

Assessment Pyramid

6b

Determine whether events are dependent or independent and find the probabilities.

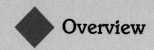

Overview

Goals and Assessment

In the *Mathematics in Context* curriculum, unit goals, organized according to levels of reasoning described in the Assessment Pyramid on page xiv, relate to the strand goals and the NCTM *Principles and Standards for School Mathematics*. The *Mathematics in Context* curriculum is designed to help students demonstrate their understanding of mathematics in each of the categories listed below.

Ongoing assessment opportunities are also indicated on their respective pages throughout the teacher guide by an assessment pyramid icon. It is important to note that the attainment of goals in one category is not a prerequisite to attaining those in another category. In fact, students should progress simultaneously toward several goals in different categories. The Goals and Assessment table is designed to support preparation of an assessment plan.

	Goal	Ongoing Assessment Opportunities		Unit Assessment Opportunities	
Level I: Conceptual and Procedural Knowledge	**1.** Use chance trees, counting strategies, two-way tables, and rules to find probability.	**Section B** **Section C** **Section D** **Section E**	p.13, #2b p. 19, #17c p. 27, #10abd p. 34, #8ab p. 37, #17a p. 42, #8abc p. 43, #10ab p. 44, #11	**Quiz 1** #2c **Quiz 2** #2ab **Test** #3a , 4ac	
	2. Use different representations (ratios, percents, fractions, and so on) to describe probability.	**Section B** **Section C** **Section D** **Section E**	p. 18, #12, 13 p. 27, #10bd p. 34, #8ab p. 44, #11	**Quiz 2** #2ab **Test** #4a	
	3. Understand that variability is inherent in any probability situation.	**Section A**	p. 3, #4abcde	**Quiz 1** #2c **Quiz 2** #2c	
	4. Use graphs and measures of central tendency to describe data.	**Section C**	p. 25, #2a, 5 p. 27, #7a p. 28, #12a	**Quiz 2** #1ab	

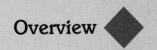
	Goal	Ongoing Assessment Opportunities	Unit Assessment Opportunities
Level II: Reasoning, Communicating, Thinking, and Making Connections	**5.** Reason about likely and unlikely samples and factors that can bias a survey.	**Section A** p. 6, #7c p. 7, #8b p. 8, #12 **Section D** p. 36, #14b	**Quiz 1** #1ab, 2a **Quiz 2** #1c **Test** #2
	6. Use simulation and modeling to investigate probability.	**Section E** p. 41, #5abc	
	7. Understand the relationship between a sample and a population and the effect of the sample size.	**Section A** p. 6, #7c	
	8. Make decisions using probability and expected values.	**Section B** p. 18, #14 **Section D** p. 34, #8cd p. 36, #14b p. 37, #17b	**Quiz 1** #2c **Quiz 2** #2d **Test** #4bc
	9. Determine whether events are dependent or independent and find the probabilities.	**Section B** p. 15, #6b p. 19, #18ab	**Quiz 1** #2b **Test** #1, 3b

	Goal	Ongoing Assessment Opportunities	Unit Assessment Opportunities
Level III: Modeling, Generalizing, and Non-Routine Problem Solving	**10.** Develop and use a critical attitude toward the use of probability.	**Section E** p. 46, #16, 18	

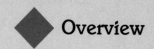
Materials Preparation

The following items are the necessary materials and resources to be used by the teacher and students throughout the unit. For further details, see the Section Overviews and the Materials section at the top of the Hints and Comments column of each teacher page. Note: Some contexts and problems can be enhanced through the use of optional materials. These optional materials are listed in the corresponding Hints and Comments column.

Student Resources

Quantities listed are per student.

- **Letter to the Family**
- **Student Activity Sheets 1–3**

Teacher Resources

- **At least 200 fish data cards (see template for cards in the Student Activity Sheet section)**

Student Materials

Quantities listed are per student, unless otherwise noted.

- **Two different-colored number cubes**

BRITANNICA

Mathematics in Context

Student Material and Teaching Notes

◆ Contents

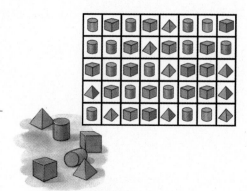

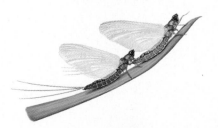

Dear Student,

Welcome to Great Predictions!

Surveys report that teens prefer brand-name jeans over any other jeans.

Do you think you can believe all the conclusions that are reported as "survey results"? How can the results be true if they are based on the responses of just a few people?

In this unit, you will investigate how statistics can help you study, and answer, those questions. As you explore the activities in this unit, watch for articles in newspapers and magazines about surveys. Bring them to class and discuss how the ideas of this unit help you interpret the surveys.

When you finish *Great Predictions*, you will appreciate how people use statistics to interpret surveys and make decisions.

Sincerely,

The Mathematics in Context Development Team

Section Focus

Students investigate chance and expected outcomes in several real world situations. They discover that drawing conclusions from samples always involves uncertainty. Students consider how samples should be taken to be able to draw reliable conclusions. They study situations in which samples give unusual results, and they reflect on whether there is a cause for these unexpected outcomes or whether they may be due to chance.

Pacing and Planning

Day 1: Chance or Not?		Student pages 1–4
INTRODUCTION	Problem 1	Discuss how a sample of the total number of households in a community is surveyed to determine the popularity of television programs.
CLASSWORK	Problems 2–4	Determine whether or not the death rate of trees dying in several forests is due to chance or another cause.
HOMEWORK	Problem 5	Consider situations where the unexpected outcome may be due to chance or to some other cause.

Day 2: Taking Samples		Student pages 4–6
ACTIVITY	Activity, page 4	Complete an experiment that involves taking samples from a population.
CLASSWORK	Problem 6	Evaluate how well samples reflect the makeup of a population.
HOMEWORK	Problem 7	Consider the reliability of samples and classify eight given samples according to the population from which they were most likely to have come.

Day 3: Taking Samples (Continued)		Student pages 7 and 8
INTRODUCTION	Problem 8	Analyze results from a survey to determine the yogurt flavor to order for the whole school.
CLASSWORK	Problems 9–11	Use the response of a representative sample to determine expected attendance.
HOMEWORK	Problem 12	Explain why a survey conducted at a school is not representative of the school population.

Teachers Matter A

Day 4: Populations and Sampling (Continued)		Student pages 9–11
INTRODUCTION	Review homework.	Review homework from Day 3.
ASSESSMENT	Problem 13; Check Your Work	Student self-assessment: Make decisions based on the analysis of survey results.
ASSESSMENT	For Further Reflection	Propose a theory about professional sampling methods.

Additional Resources: Additional Practice, Section A, Student Book page 50

Materials

Student Resources

Quantities listed are per student.

- Letter to the Family
- **Student Activity Sheet 1**

Teachers Resources

No resources required

Student Materials

No resources required

* See Hints and Comments for optional materials.

Learning Lines

Sample and Population

In this section, the terms sample and population are important concepts. These were introduced and used in the unit *Dealing with Data* and further elaborated and used in the units *Insights into Data* and *Second Chance*. In this section they are revisited and formalized. Students use results from samples to make estimates about the population using ratios and percents. They investigate several real-life situations, such as television ratings, surveys for favorite music, and attendance in the House of Representatives.

Students consider how reliable the estimates for the population are, whether the sampling process was biased, and if unexpected results may be due to chance or other factors. Students understand that sampling needs to be random, representative, and not selective (e.g., only asking friends). A sample also needs to be of sufficient size.

Students also realize that, in real-life situations, other information than the information collected by sampling may be needed to make a decision about a situation.

Sample and Simulation

Students select random samples from a population of 400 colored and white squares. The squares are a model of the real-life situation and students simulate taking samples. In the simulation students can take as many random samples as they like and as large a sample as they like. In doing so, students discover that sampling always involves uncertainty and there is variability in the results. By taking several samples or by increasing the sample size, the chance of getting unexpected and unusual results gets smaller and the results will better reflect the population.

At the End of This Section: Learning Outcomes

Students have a better understanding of the relationship between a sample and a population. They can draw conclusions from samples, and they know that uncertainty or chance is involved when doing this. They are also aware of methods to reduce this uncertainty. Students know that samples must be large enough and randomly selected to give representative results for the population.

Notes

This page introduces the first context, television ratings, and begins to introduce the idea of the section, using samples to make conclusions.

Some students may have been part of a "Nielsen Family" and be able to share what they had to do. Some families fill out a diary while others have a device attached to their television set.

Drawing Conclusions from Samples

Chance or Not?

How Do Television Networks Rate Their Programs?

People often complain about the number of commercials aired during their favorite television program, but the money brought in by these commercials pays the majority of the cost of producing the program. The cost of airing a commercial during a television program largely depends on the current rating of the program. Popular television programs often charge top dollar for a one-minute commercial spot, while less popular programs charge less money. Therefore, television networks look closely at each program's rating on a weekly basis.

The rating for a particular show is the percent of households with TVs that watch the show. How do the major television networks determine who is watching what program?

Reaching All Learners

Vocabulary Building

The term *rating* is defined in the text, it is important that students realize that the rating is expressed in terms of a percent.

English Language Learners

There is a great deal of text on this page; partner reading or reading aloud with the whole class may be particularly useful for English language learners.

Hints and Comments

Overview

Students read a text about how TV ratings are determined by large samples of people who record the television programs they watch weekly. There are no problems for students to solve on this page.

About the Mathematics

In this context, the concepts of sampling, population, representativeness, and bias are informally revisited. These topics were formally introduced in the unit *Insights into Data*.

Planning

You may want to discuss the text in class before proceeding to problem 1 on the next page, Student Book page 2. For more information on TV ratings and how data are collected, see, for example: http://www.nielsenmedia.com/

You may also have students do this problem first and have a class discussion following that. When you discuss this text and problem 1, you may want to refer to the unit *Insights into Data* to review the concepts of sampling, representativeness, and bias.

Did You Know?

Student interest in the Nielson ratings is usually quite high. Some students in your class might have been part of a sample, either keeping a diary or having a monitor attached to their television at home. The ratings are important, not only because they reflect how many people watch a given program, but also because they reflect who watches the program. Young people spend more money than older people, so programs that are watched primarily by older people are sometimes dropped, even though there is a large audience, because the audience does not spend enough to make the ads profitable.

A Drawing Conclusions from Samples

Notes

1 Students may refer back to earlier units where they have learned about sampling, representativeness, and bias.

1d Students should mention that there will be some variability in the estimates due to the sampling process and that the sample may not have exactly the same characteristics as the whole population. At this time, students are not expected to use the terms *sampling, population,* or *bias.*

2b Students should realize that while some difference from an average may be expected, this difference is quite substantial.

At one time, independent survey companies asked a large sample of people to complete a diary in which they listed all the programs they watched each week. For example, in a city with 297,970 households with TVs, the survey company might have 463 households keep diaries.

1. **a.** Why didn't survey companies give a diary to every household?

   b. How do you think survey results could be used to estimate the overall popularity of television programs?

   c. Suppose that 230 of the 463 surveyed households watched the Super Bowl. How would you estimate the total number of households in that city that watched the Super Bowl?

   d. How reliable do you think the estimate would be?

A Forest at Risk

In a forested area near Snow Creek, an average of 12 trees per 10 acres died from severe weather conditions over the last several years. But this year from January to August, forest rangers reported about 42 dead or dying trees per 10 acres.

2. **a.** The forest near Snow Creek is about 5,000 acres. How many trees would you normally expect to die from storms in the area?

   b. Explain whether you think the foresters should be concerned about the health of the trees.

Many insects and diseases are an important part of creating healthy and diverse patterns of vegetation in the forests, even though they sometimes kill or stunt large patches of trees. In addition, trees are often stressed by weather conditions (too much or too little water, for example) and die.

In many areas of the Rocky Mountains, the forest rangers found clusters of trees scattered throughout the forests that were dying. They discovered that the trees were infested by a beetle that burrows into the bark.

Reaching All Learners

Accommodation

Encourage students who are struggling to use a ratio table to solve problem 2a.

Extension

Have students look up the ratings for particular TV shows and then compare the ratings to the number of families represented in the class who watched the show.

Solutions and Samples

1. a. Answers will vary. Sample response:

It would be very expensive and time-consuming to have everyone who watches television keep a diary. Many people would refuse to keep a diary or might not keep accurate records.

b. Answers will vary. Sample response:

The popularity of television programs is estimated by calculating the percent of the people in the sample who watched a particular show and then using that to estimate the percent of the whole population that might be watching the show.

c. Answers will vary. Accept answers close to 150,000. Students may use a variety of strategies to solve this problem.

Students might reason as follows:

$\frac{230}{463}$ is about $\frac{230}{460}$ which is $\frac{1}{2}$. So about one-half of 297,970 households in the city, or approximately 149,000 households, were watching the Super Bowl.

d. Answers will vary. Sample response:

It depends on whether the 463 households fairly represent all the people in the city. If the group was randomly selected, the estimate is probably fairly reliable.

2. a. About 6,000 trees. Students might reason as follows: 12 trees per 10 acres is 1,200 trees per 1,000 acres, so $1,200 \times 5 = 6,000$ trees per 5,000 acres.

b. Answers will vary. Sample responses:

- Yes, because in eight months, more than three times the normal average of trees died. So the foresters should be concerned and further investigate the situation.

- No, because 12 trees per 10 acres is an average. The actual number of trees dying per year can be different. You do not know how many years this average represents. So the foresters should not be concerned.

Hints and Comments

Overview

Students reflect on the method television networks use to rate their programs. Next they are introduced to the situation of trees dying in several forests. Students consider whether this may be due to chance or to another cause.

About the Mathematics

In the case of collecting information to rate television programs, the population at study is very large; therefore, sample(s) need to be taken. If the sample is representative and large enough, the results will be reliable for smaller samples. Large variation in the results may occur due to chance. Based on the results of a sample, estimations can be made for the whole population. Students will do so using ratios or percents. Students consider causes for unexpected events in a sample. If results are unexpected or unusual, this can be due to several reasons: it can be "pure chance," the sample may not be "good" or be too small, or there may be other causes. In problem 2, students informally calculate an expected value. This concept will be formalized later in the unit.

Planning

Students may work on problems 1 and 2 individually or in small groups. You may want to discuss their explanations for 1d and 2b. See also suggestions on the previous page.

Comments About the Solutions

1. c. Students should understand that the percent in the sample is only an estimate of the percent for the population. Students may use several strategies to solve this problem. You may want to discuss these in class, possibly in combination with the strategies for this problem.

2. a. Students may use several strategies; even with a ratio table, different operations may be used. You may want to discuss these in class, possibly in combination with the strategies for problem 2c.

b. Encourage students to provide sound reasoning. You may want to ask them what assumptions underlie their answers.

Drawing Conclusions from Samples

Notes

3a This problem may provide a good connection to the science class as students think about possible differences.

3b Encourage students to be specific in their descriptions of what foresters might do.

The mountain pine beetle is the most aggressive and destructive insect affecting pine trees in western North America. Pine beetles are part of the natural cycle in forests. Recent evidence indicates that in certain regions, mountain pine beetle populations are on the rise.

In the Rocky Mountains, more trees were dying than was normally expected.

3. **a.** **Reflect** The number of dead or dying trees seemed to be different in certain areas, for example in Snow Creek and the Rocky Mountains. What may have caused this difference?

   b. What do you think foresters do to support their case that the change in the number of damaged and dying trees is something to watch?

There is a similarity between the two examples presented in questions 2 and 3. In each case, an important question is being raised.

When is a difference from an expected outcome a coincidence (or due to chance), and when could there be another explanation that needs to be investigated?

Keep this question in mind throughout this section as you look at other situations. For the example about Snow Creek, the high number of death or dying trees seemed to be a coincidence, while there seemed to be an explanation for the high rate of dying trees in the Rocky Mountains.

For each of the following situations, the result may be due to chance or perhaps there is another explanation. For each situation, give an explanation other than chance. Then decide which cause you think is more likely, your explanation or chance.

4. **a.** A basketball player made eleven free throws in a row.

   b. Each of the last seven cars that drove past a school was red.

   c. In your town, the sun has not been out for two weeks.

   d. On the drive to school one morning, all the traffic lights were green.

   e. All of the winners of an elementary school raffle were first-graders.

Assessment Pyramid

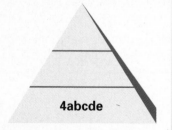

4abcde

Understand that variability is inherent in any probability situation.

Reaching All Learners

Extension

Encourage students to check newspapers and magazines for articles about "lucky streaks," unusually warm weather for a long period of time, or other unusual occurrences. Discuss whether these are truly unusual and whether they might have occurred by chance or could have been caused by some other factor.

Solutions and Samples

3. a. It is suggested that the larger number of dying trees in the Rocky Mountains is caused by the fact that the number of mountain pine beetles is on the rise. It is not clear whether this is also the case in Snow Creek forest. The larger number of dying trees may be due to chance. It is also possible other factors are causing this.

b. Answers may differ. Sample answer:

The foresters should present information on the numbers of trees dying for several years and make clear that the number is now unusually high. They may use tables or graphs or a map of the forest to support this. In addition, they may research the number of mountain pine beetles in the area to see if the number is rising.

4. Explanations will vary. Sample explanations:

a. The basketball player may have been lucky, but it is more likely that he or she is a very good shooter.

b. Maybe the cars belong to a club or organization, but it is more likely that it was a coincidence.

c. The overcast skies may be the result of major climatic changes, normal weather patterns, or chance.

d. It may be luck that the traffic lights were all green, but it is more likely that the lights were all timed so that someone driving at a constant speed could make all the green lights without stopping.

e. It may be coincidence that all the winners were first-graders, or perhaps many more first-graders entered the school raffle.

Hints and Comments

Overview

Students continue their investigation of the dying trees in several areas, they reflect on the possible causes of unexpected outcomes: due to chance or not?

About the Mathematics

The situation described on the previous page and the situation described here both deal with an unexpected event, a number of dying trees higher than normal. In the first situation — in Snow Creek—, this may have been due to chance, and in the second situation — the Rocky Mountains—, other factors are seen to contribute to this high number. Investigations into possible causes may be needed if other factors seem to have caused the unusual and unexpected outcomes. Problems 2 and 3 deal informally with expected value, and implicit attention is paid to the fact that a sample does not always reflect the population.

Planning

You may want students to work on problems 3 and 4 individually. Have students compare their answers for problems 2 and 3.

Comments About the Solutions

3. Students can find information regarding this question in the text on Student Book pages 2 and 3. They may also look for other information on this subject on the Internet, for example.

A Drawing Conclusions from Samples

Notes

Be sure that students understand that the entire square represents the population and the colored squares are randomly colored to represent the newspaper subscribers.

Activity

Students could also do this activity by dropping a small opened paper clip. Where the open point of the paper clip lands would be where they look to keep the tally.

 5. **Reflect** If something unusual happened in your life, how would you decide whether it was due to chance or something else? Give an example.

Taking Samples

Here are some terms that are helpful when you want to talk about chance.

A **population** is the whole group in which you are interested.

A **sample** is a part of that population.

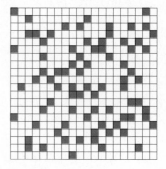

In a town of 400 people, 80 subscribe to the local newspaper. This could be represented in a diagram in which 80 out of 400 squares have been filled in randomly. So the red squares represent the subscribers.

A researcher wants to take a random sample of ten people from the population in the town. You are going to simulate taking the sample by using the diagram on **Student Activity Sheet 1**.

Activity

Close your eyes and hold your pencil over the diagram on **Student Activity Sheet 1**. Let the tip of your pencil land lightly on the diagram. Open your eyes and note where the tip landed.

Do this experiment a total of 10 times, keeping track of how many times you land on a black square. The 10 squares that you land on are a sample.

Reaching All Learners

Vocabulary Building

Both *population* and *sample* are defined on this page. It is important that students understand, and are comfortable using, both of these terms correctly.

Writing Opportunity

This problem can be used as part of a whole-class activity in which students write, present, and discuss personal experiences with unexpected events. You might have students write their answers in the form of a small story describing an unexpected event in their notebooks. Students may read their stories in class. After each story, you might lead the whole class in a discussion of a likely explanation for the unexpected event.

Solutions and Samples

5. Answers will vary. Sample response:

If something unusual happened to me, I would find out what the chances were for this event to randomly occur. The event might happen due to something that was planned. It might be that I got a really good test grade in a subject I find difficult (I could have really studied or just guessed and been lucky), or that all of my friends and I wore the same color shirt to school (we all belonged to the band and it was band day, or it was just coincidental).

Hints and Comments

Materials

Student Activity Sheet 1 (one per student); graphing calculator, optional (one per student)

Overview

Students perform an experiment in which they take samples from a population by randomly choosing squares from a diagram.

About the Mathematics

The relationship between the distribution of a population and that of a sample is explored in this activity. This issue is also covered in the unit *Insights into Data*. A random sample is one in which every member of the population has an equal chance of being selected and the selection of one member does not affect the selection of another. Students are supposed to take random samples in the activity. But it will probably be difficult to obtain a truly random sample because students will tend to select squares from the middle of the chart.

Planning

Students will do the activity individually. Make sure they record the results. You may want to have students take a bigger sample, for example 25 tries.

Extension or Alternative Using Technology

It is possible to use a graphing calculator to simulate the situation. Students can use a calculator simulation to look at a larger sample. Say, *In a calculator simulation, you will use dots instead of squares to represent your population. Working in small groups, use the directions on the activity sheet to create a population of 400 dots, 80 of which are marked. From this population, you will take a sample of 25 dots and display it on your calculator.*

1. Each student should select a different sample of 25 from the population and record the number of marked dots in that sample. Note: Each member of the group selects a different sample of 25 dots, but all members use the same population.

    a. How many marked dots would you expect in your sample of 25? (answer: about 5)

    b. Look at the numbers of marked dots in the samples from your group. Which, if any, of the samples would you call unexpected? Why do you think they are unexpected? (sample answer: 10, which is 40% or higher, can be called unexpected)

See more Hints and Comments on page 91.

Drawing Conclusions from Samples

Notes

6 This series of questions allows students to begin thinking informally about the chance, then calculating the theoretical probability, and then looking at the experimental probability. While it is not necessary that students know these terms, it may be useful to have a conversation with the students about the progression of the questions.

6. a. Do you think that, in general, there is a better chance of landing on a white square or on a black square?

b. What is the chance (probability) of landing on a black square? How did you calculate the chance?

c. Organize the samples from the entire class in a chart like the one shown.

d. Look carefully at the chart below and describe what this tells you about the random samples. How well do the samples reflect the overall population with respect to the subscribers to the newspaper?

Number of Black Squares in 10 Tries	Number of Students Who Get This Number
0	
1	
2	
3	
4	
5	
6	
7	
8	
9	
10	

Reaching All Learners

Accommodation

It may be helpful to prepare a histogram that can be filled in to graphically represent the chart.

Solutions and Samples

6. a. Answers will vary. Sample response:

Chances are better that the pencil will fall on a white square since there are 320 white squares and only 80 black squares.

b. The chance is one-fifth, or 20%. Strategies will vary. The chance can be found by dividing the number of black squares by the total number of squares; 80 divided by 400 is $\frac{80}{400}$, which is $\frac{1}{5}$, or 20%. It can also be found by converting 80 out of 400 to 20 out of 100, which is 20%.

c. Results will vary. Sample result of 19 students:

Number of Black Squares in 10 Tries	0	1	2	3	4	5	6	7	8	9	10
Number of Students Who Get This Number	0	2	8	5	2	1	0	1	0	0	0

d. Answers will vary, depending on the collected results. Sample response based on the sample results for part **c**:

Eight people's pencils landed on a black square in 2 out of 10 trials. This means the most common result is that 2 out of 10 people subscribed to the newspaper, which is 20%. You could expect an answer like this because of the way reasoned for the answer to part **b**. This was the most likely result for the experiment. However, five people's pencils landed on a black square in 3 out of 10 trials, and others had results that were farther away from two out of 10. All of these were by chance.

Hints and Comments

Materials

transparency of chart shown on Student Book page 5, optional (one per class);
overhead projector, optional (one per class)

Overview

Students investigate how well their samples reflect the makeup of the population.

About the Mathematics

Students were introduced to finding chance as a ratio of the number of favorable outcomes divided by the total number of possible outcomes in the unit *Second Chance*. Students should be able to convert and move easily between the different representations of chance: ratios, fractions, percents, and decimals. In the activity, the sample size is small (only 10). If samples from the whole class are collected, the distribution will become clear.

Planning

Students may work on parts **a** and **b** individually. Part **c** will be a whole class activity. Part **d** can be done individually again. Discuss the answers to part **d**, in class.

Comments About the Solutions

6. b. Chance can best be found by starting with a ratio and converting this into a percent or fraction. Calculating chance is also addressed in the units *Take a Chance* and *Second Chance*.

c. Collect the results on the activity from the entire class. This can be done in a chart on the board or an overhead projector.

d. Students should realize that not all random samples are equivalent; a sample can be a good sample even though it does not have exactly the same ratio of marked squares as the population. The variation is due to chance.

It can be difficult to draw a conclusion about a population from a sample. Consider the following problem, in which members of a population are represented by squares.

Each of the samples was taken from one of three different populations. Population A has 200 red squares out of 1,000. Population B has 300 red squares out of 1,000, and Population C has 500 red squares out of 1,000.

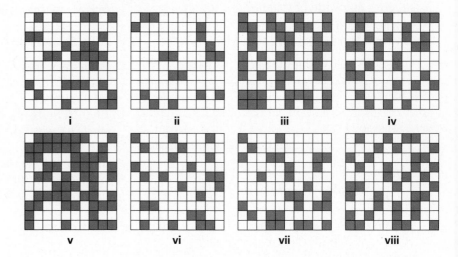

i   ii   iii   iv

v   vi   vii   viii

7 Encourage students to decide which population each sample comes from by estimating the percent of shaded squares, rather than by counting. Challenge the students by asking, *Could all of the samples come from the same population?* **They could, but it is not likely since some are quite different from others.**

7. a. For each sample, decide whether you think it belongs to Population A, Population B, or Population C. Explain why you made each decision. What is the size of each sample?

b. Which samples do you find the most difficult to classify? Why are these difficult?

c. What do you think is the problem with making a conclusion based on a sample?

Assessment Pyramid

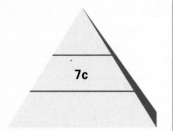

7c

Reason about likely and unlikely samples. Understand the relationship between a sample and a population.

Reaching All Learners

Intervention

This is the point where it is critical that students understand that samples usually represent their population accurately, but there is some variation. If students are unclear about this, you could conduct an experiment drawing different colored chips from a bag. Hopefully, students will begin to see that most samples are similar to the population, but some variation is expected.

Accommodation

You may want to make three "parent populations", labeled A, B, and C, on transparencies with 1,000-square grids with 200, 300, and 500 squares shaded to help students visualize the populations.

Solutions and Samples

7. a. Answers will vary. Sample response:

  i   is from population B (with 28 red squares out of 100);

  ii is from population A (with 17 red squares out of 100);

  iii is from population C (with with 47 red squares out of 100);

  iv is from population B (with 33 red squares out of 100);

  v   is from population C (with 57 red squares out of 100);

  vi may come from population A or population B (with 24 red squares out of 100);

  vii is from population B (with 28 red squares out of 100);

  viii may come from population B or population C (with 38 red squares out of 100).

b. Answers will vary. Sample response:

The most difficult samples to classify are **vi** and **viii**, because the ratio of red squares to the total falls between the ratios for two different populations.

c. Answers will vary. Sample response:

The problem with drawing conclusions based on samples is that, by chance, a sample may be very different from the population.

Hints and Comments

Materials

blank transparencies, optional (three per class); overhead projector, optional (one per class)

Overview

Students consider the reliability of samples and classify eight given samples according to the population from which they were most likely to have come.

About the Mathematics

Samples, even if they are representative and large enough, may not reflect the overall population with respect to the aspects studied. The eight samples on this page are taken 'literally' from the parent populations. There are no unknown factors nor redundant information since the situation is just about red and white squares. This will provide a clearer picture of the relation between samples and populations. Still for some samples, it is hard to decide from which population they have been taken. This is due to chance, to variability. There is no other cause in this case!

Planning

Students may work on problem 6 in small groups. Encourage students to discuss this problem. After students complete it, you may want to briefly discuss it as a whole-class activity.

Comments about the Problems

7. Encourage students to decide which population each sample comes from by estimating the percent of red squares, rather than by counting. Ask, *Could samples VI and VIII come from the same population?* [Yes, such different samples could come from the same population.]

Again students should realize that not all random samples are equivalent; a sample can be a good sample even though it does not have exactly the same ratio of marked squares as the population. The variation is due to chance.

A Drawing Conclusions from Samples

Notes

8a With the number of students who were asked given, it should be easy for students to find out how many made each choice.

8b It is important for students to realize that Tara's is not a representative sample.

10 Students should think about possible sources of bias that might occur even in this situation.

Who Prefers Which Yogurt?

Tara is trying to determine whether students at her school prefer vanilla, banana, or strawberry yogurt. She asks four friends and records their preferences. Based on their preferences Tara decides that half the school prefers strawberry, 25% prefer vanilla, and 25% prefer banana.

Carla is interested in the same question. She stands at the door as students are leaving school and asks 50 students which flavor they prefer. She decides that 22% prefer strawberry, 26% prefer vanilla, and 52% prefer banana.

8. a. How did Tara and Carla come up with the percentages?

b. Reflect If you were ordering the yogurt for the school picnic, on whose results would you base your order, Tara's or Carla's? Why?

Who's Going to the Zoo?

Suppose you are the director of a zoo and you are having students in the area attend the grand opening of a new primate center.

There are five schools in your area, each with 300–500 students, but you know that not every student will be able to attend. You randomly choose 20 students from each school and ask whether they would be interested in attending. Your survey results suggest that 30 students say that they will attend, and 70 students say that they will not attend.

9. a. If 2,000 students live in the area, how many would you expect to come to the grand opening?

b. Reflect To plan the grand opening, what else do you need to know?

In the zoo problem, you could not know the percent of students in the population who would attend, so you needed a sample to estimate the percent.

10. To answer problem 9a, you probably assumed that the sample and the population had the same percentage of students who wanted to attend the opening. How reasonable is this assumption?

Assessment Pyramid

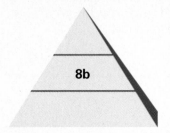

8b

Reason about likely and unlikely samples and factors that can bias a survey.

Reaching All Learners

Extension

Students could be challenged to come up with a survey for your school and to explain both a sample that would be unlikely to yield useful results and a sample that would be more reliable.

Solutions and Samples

8. a. Answers will vary. Sample response.

Tara asked four friends. If she concludes that 50% like strawberry, two of her friends must have liked strawberry, since 2 out of 4 is 50%. Tara then concluded that 50% of the whole school would prefer strawberry. She did the same for vanilla and banana. Each flavor was preferred by one of her four friends; 1 out of 4 is 25%.

Carla asked 50 students. She concludes 22% prefer strawberry; this would most likely mean that 22% out of the 50 students he asked (11 students) said they liked strawberry best. The same for the other flavors: 26% of the 50, which is 13 students, preferred vanilla, and the rest, 26 students (52% out of 50) preferred banana.

b. Answers will vary. Sample response:

- I would base the school's order on Carla's results because she surveyed a larger sample of students.

- I would use Carlas's results because Tara only asked her friends and they might not be typical of any of the other students. Carla at least used a method that might get opinions from all different sets of students.

9. a. Answers will vary. Sample response:

Out of 2,000 students, about 600 are expected to attend the opening at the zoo. This is 30% of 2,000. Since in the sample there are 20 students selected from 5 schools, the sample is 100 students. Thirty out of 100 say they will attend the opening, which is 30%.

	×10	×2
Students Attending	30	300	600
Total Number of Students	100	1,000	2,000

The actual number of students attending may vary a bit around 600 because the sample will not quite approximate the total population.

b. Answers will vary. Sample response:

The zoo director needs to know, for example, what time the students will arrive, how the group will be supervised, and whether the students plan to eat lunch at the zoo.

Hints and Comments

Overview

Students decide which sample they will base their decisions about the yogurt flavor to order for the whole school. Next they draw conclusions based on the response of a representative sample about the number of students expected to attend the opening of a new primate center.

About the Mathematics

When conclusions are based on samples, it is important to know how the sampling process has been done and whether there are possible causes for bias. Students should further develop and use a critical attitude towards sampling and drawing conclusions. Students were informally introduced to the concepts of population and sampling in the units *Take a Chance* and *Second Chance*, this was formalized and connected to the concept of bias in the unit *Insights into Data*. Students should be able to calculate easily with ratios and percents.

Planning

Students may work on problems 8–10 in small groups. You may want to discuss students' answers to problem 10 in class.

Comments About the Solutions

8. Make sure students understand that the percentages in the text are based on the answers of the students in the samples. They should also understand the need to reason backwards from the statements about the population (the whole school) to the samples (of 4 students and of 50 students).

10. Answers will vary. Sample response:

It is risky to assume that calculating the ratio of those who will attend from a single sample will give the same ratio as those from the population who will attend. Unusual samples can occur by chance. Other samples may produce slightly different results. On the other hand, the sample seems to be drawn in a way that gives all students a chance to be selected: 20 students are randomly chosen from each of the five schools, and each school is about the same size. So it is likely that the sample percent is somewhat close to the population percent.

A Drawing Conclusions from Samples

Notes

Who Was in the House?

The illustration represents the U.S. House of Representatives during a session. The House has 435 members. You can see from the empty chairs that some members were missing.

11. **a.** Explain why the illustration represents a sample of the members of the U.S. House of Representatives.

    b. You may assume that this sample is randomly chosen. How many members do you think attended the session?

Populations and Sampling

What Kind of Music Do You Like?

Natasha and David think that the school should play music in the cafeteria during lunch. The principal agrees that it is a good idea and tells David and Natasha to find out what kind of music the students want. The two decide to survey the students in their next classes and also to ask anyone else they happen to meet in the halls. Natasha goes to band class, and David goes to his computer class. Natasha and David present the results of their survey to the principal.

12. Write a brief note to the principal explaining why the results of the survey of Natasha and David should not be used to make a decision about what kind of music to play in the cafeteria.

11 You may want to make a transparency of the picture on Student Book page 8 and use it to discuss the problem. You can write numbers in the seats, and shade empty seats a different color than occupied seats. Encourage students to explain whether they think the given sample is good or bad, and why.

12 This problem can be connected to the language arts class if writing a business letter is a skill in that curriculum.

Assessment Pyramid

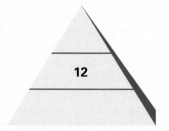

Reason about likely and unlikely samples and factors that can bias a survey.

Reaching All Learners

Accommodation

Some students may need to first count the number of chairs and number of people and record that information before moving to problem 11b.

Extension

You may want to have students look for examples of surveys that are biased. You might bring in, or have students bring in, a report about a poll. Students could write a description of the sampling process and the questions that were asked and explain whether or not they think the results might be biased.

Solutions and Samples

11. a. Explanations will vary. Sample explanations:

- The illustration represents a sample because not all of the seats for the 435 representatives are visible.

- It is a sample of the members of the U.S. House of Representatives because the illustration shows a part of it.

b. Answers will vary. About 290 members probably attended the session. 300 can also be a good enough estimate. Sample strategy:
Count the members in the illustration (20) and the empty seats (10), and use the same proportion for the 435 members of the full House; $\frac{20}{30}$, or $\frac{2}{3}$ of 435 is 290 people who attended.

A ratio table may be used as well; Sample ratio table:

$$\times 10 \qquad \div 2 \qquad \times 3$$

Members Attending	20	200	100	300
Total Number of Seats	30	300	150	450

So an estimate is that 300 members attended.

12. Letters will vary. Students' letters should include the argument that it is likely that the sample that Natasha and David used represents only a small part of the school population. Natasha and David asked people in only two specialized classes—band and computer—and the people they "met in the halls," probably their friends. This sample may not represent the views of most students. Also, students in band class may prefer other types of music from students who are not in band class.

Hints and Comments

Materials

transparency of illustration on Student Book page 8, optional (one per class);
overhead projector, optional (one per class)

Overview

Students estimate how many representatives in the U.S. House of Representatives attended a session, based on an illustration of part of the House floor. Next students explain why a survey conducted at a school is not representative of the whole school population.

About the Mathematics

Students revisit the concept of the representativeness of samples of the population. In one example, the sample is presented visually, students need to retrieve the numerical information from the illustration. To do so, they need to decide which aspects of the illustration are relevant and how the illustration forms a sample.

Planning

Students may work on problems 11 and 12 in small groups.

Comments About the Solutions

12. Encourage students to think about how the process used to select the samples could produce a biased sample. This kind of a sample is usually referred to as a convenience sample and may give biased results, representing the views of only one part of the population.

Drawing Conclusions from Samples

Notes

At this point, students should be quite comfortable with the idea of sampling and be able to evaluate claims based on a sample.

13a and b It is important that students understand the difference between the population and the sample in this article.

13d Two aspects should be discussed: the fact that the people in the study get older as well as the fact that technologies tend to spread over more groups over time. This is hinted at in the last paragraph of the article.

NEWS WATCH: DATA POINT;

For the Music Lover, Gray Hair Is No Barrier to White Earbuds

By MARK GLASSMAN
Published: February 17, 2005

Youthful silhouettes rocking out may be the new fresh faces of portable digital music, but—shh!—grown-ups are listening, too.

Roughly one in nine Americans 18 or older has an iPod or an MP3 player, according to survey results released this week by the Pew Internet and American Life Project.

Younger adults were the most likely group to own the devices. Roughly one in five people 18 to 28 years old said they had a music player. About 2 percent of those 69 and over reported owning one.

"It's obviously just now reaching the tipping point as a technology," Lee Rainie, the project director, said of digital music players. "I would think that we'll even have accelerating growth over the next year or two." He said more adults would probably buy the devices "as more players come into the market; as the price point rolls down; as Apple itself rolls out new products."

The survey, drawing on responses of 2,201 people by telephone, also revealed a small gender gap, with more men (14 percent) owning the devices than women (9 percent). "Look at any technology deployment over the last century and a half," Mr. Rainie said. "Men tend to be dominant early on, and women tend to catch up."

Source: *New York Times*, February 17, 2005

---

13. **a.** What population was studied in the article?

 b. Describe the sample taken: do you think this is a good sample? Why or why not?

 c. Do you think you can believe the claim made in the second paragraph of the article: "Roughly one in nine Americans 18 or older has an iPod or an MP3 player." Explain your reasoning.

 d. How do you think the results will be different if this study were to be repeated 5 years from now?

Reaching All Learners

Accommodation

Provide students with a copy of the article so that they can underline or highlight key information.

Extension

Ask students to locate the reporting of the results of another survey in the newspaper. They can answer parts **a** and **b** in relation to this survey and then comment on it.

It is possible to look for information on the Internet about the number of people who own technological devices (for different years). For example, information on cellular phone ownership can be easily found.

Solutions and Samples

13. a. The population being studied was Americans of 18 years or older. This is mentioned in the second paragraph of the article.

b. Answers will vary. They may contain the following elements:

- The responses are from 2,201 people, and the survey is taken by telephone. See the last paragraph of the article.

- There is no information given on the actual sampling process.

- It is clear that women as well as men were in the sample and that different age groups were represented in the sample.

- It is unclear whether the respondents were selected randomly, in a way that mirrors the population distribution with respect to a certain variable.

- It is also unclear if all persons sampled actually responded. Probably not, since 2,201 seems like a strange number to take as a sample size.

c. Answers will vary. Some students may doubt the claim because they believe that the sample of 2,201 people is not large enough to represent all Americans 18 years or over.

Other students may be more inclined to believe the statement because they may see the sample as being typical and unbiased because it is taken by an official project.

d. Answers will vary. Some students may think that more people will own a music player because technology spreads over time. They may also reason that in 5 years all people that are now in the study will still own a music player and the group of 18–28 will have new people (that are now younger) who will then own a player as well. Other students may think that in five years there will be different devices, so maybe fewer will own a music player.

Hints and Comments

Overview

Students read an article presenting results of a survey on what people own music players. They explore the representativeness of the sample that was taken.

About the Mathematics

Students revisit the issue of bias in sampling. It is important they learn to have a critical attitude when reading articles or watching television programs in which results from surveys are presented. Often not enough information is given on the sampling process. This makes it hard (or impossible) to judge the value of the conclusions. Bias in sampling has been studied in the unit *Insights into Data* as well.

Planning

Students may work on problem 13 in small groups. You may want to read the article first as a whole class.

Comments About the Solutions.

13. c. The results presented cannot be used to verify the claim made that 'roughly one in nine Americans owns a music player.' Only part of the overall results are mentioned: for the age groups 18–28 and 69 and over.

Drawing Conclusions from Samples

Notes

Be sure to read the Summary as a class. One strategy is to call on students to identify the key points in the Summary and then have them refer back to the contexts in the section that illustrate the idea.

Summary

Drawing conclusions from samples always involves uncertainty.

In the case of the television ratings, it would take too much time and cost too much money to find the exact number of people who watch a certain program. Instead, information from a random sample can be used to deduce information about the whole group. By doing this, you introduce uncertainty.

Information from a sample drawn from a population may or may not be what you would expect about the population. If a sample seems unusual, you have to think about whether there could be an explanation or whether the difference is due to chance. In Snow Creek the higher number of damaged trees seemed to be due to chance, but in the Rocky Mountains the unusual high number of damaged trees could be explained by the increasing numbers of mountain pine beetles.

Sample results can be affected by the way questions are asked and the way the sample was selected.

When taking a sample, it is important to do so randomly so that every different possible sample of the size you want from the population has the same chance of being selected.

Check Your Work

Bora Middle School has a total of 250 students. A survey about pets was conducted at the school. Sixty percent of the students have one or more pets.

1. How many students in Bora Middle School have one or more pets?

Assessment Pyramid

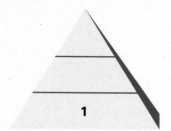

Assesses Section A Goals

Reaching All Learners

Parent Involvement

Have students share the Summary with their parents as well as their work on the Check Your Work problems. Parents will be better able to support their students by seeing where the unit begins.

Intervention

If students are struggling with problem 1, have them make a ratio table by first asking, *If there were 100 students, how many would have one or more pets?*

Solutions and Samples

1. 150 students have one or more pets.

   One solution is using the 10% strategy.

   10% of 250 = 25

   60% of 250 is 6 × 25 = 150

Hints and Comments

Overview

Students read the Summary, which reviews the main topics covered in this section.

Notes

2c Challenge students to think about many possible explanations.

3b Students should realize that this is more than the total for the whole school.

4 This problem summarizes the main idea of the unit. Have students share their answers after they have written them so that they have an opportunity to hear others' ideas.

For Further Reflection

This extends the idea of sampling from sampling the whole population to sampling subsets of the population. Be sure that students understand what is being done before they spend time thinking.

Claire asked 20 students in her sixth-grade science class if they have any pets.

2. a. How many of the 20 students do you expect answered "yes"? Explain.

b. It turned out that 16 out of the 20 students that Claire surveyed have one or more pets. Does this result surprise you? Why or why not?

c. Why do you think so many students in Claire's science class have pets?

3. a. If Claire had asked 200 students at Bora Middle School instead of 20, how many would you expect to have pets?

b. Would you be surprised if Claire told you she found that 160 out of the 200 have pets? Explain your answer.

4. Suppose you want to know how many students in your school have pets. You cannot take a survey or ask all students. In what way would you select a sample to find out how many students in your school have pets? Give reasons for your answer.

 For Further Reflection

When sampling is done to rate television programs, the poll takers do not take a random sample of the entire population. Instead they divide the population into age groups. What are some of the reasons why they might do this?

Assessment Pyramid

2, 3, 4, ☐FFR

Assesses Section A Goals

Reaching All Learners

Extension

Ask students to think of another situation when it might make sense to divide the population before taking a random sample.

Advanced Learners

Push students to use the fact that random samples can be different from the population to defend the practice of sampling from different age categories.

Solutions and Samples

2. a. The expected number of students is 12. One possible explanation: If the sample of 20 students is typical for the whole school, then you might expect 60% of 20 students, which is 12, to have one or more pets.

b. Different responses are possible. Sixteen out of 20 is not surprising since it seems to be pretty close to the expected number of 12. The four additional students having one or more pets may be due to chance.

Sixteen out of 20 is surprising since this is 80% of the sample, which seems a lot bigger than the 60% that was expected. But you should remember that a sample of size 20 is fairly small. Just a few people different from what you would expect will change the percent quite a lot, so it is really hard to say that it is not just chance.

c. Different responses are possible. Students from lower grades may be more likely to have pets. Students who take biology classes may be more likely to have pets. Perhaps Claire asked only her friends who like pets.

3. a. The expected number is 120. You can use different strategies, for example, a ratio table.

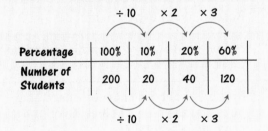

	÷ 10	× 2	× 3
Percentage	100%	10%	20%	60%
Number of Students	200	20	40	120

÷ 10   × 2   × 3

b. Yes. You might have different explanations.

1st example: I would expect that a large sample of 200 people would be more typical of the population. The number of students with pets should be close to the expected number (120).

2nd example: Only 150 students in the school have pets (see problem 1), so even if Claire asked 200 different students in the school, she could not have found 160 who had pets.

4. Different answers are possible. You may use the rolls from each grade level and randomly select a number of students from each grade. This number must not be too small. During lunch break, you might also ask every fifth student who leaves the lunch room. You can think of other methods yourself! Be sure your sample is taken at random—that means every student in your school must have the same chance of being in the sample.

Hints and Comments

Overview

In Check Your Work, students assess themselves on the concepts and skills from this section. Students can check their answers on pages 55-56 of the Student Book. They reflect on the topics addressed in this section in the problem for Further Reflection.

Planning

After students finish Section A, you may assign appropriate activities from the Additional Practice section, located on page 50 of the *Great Predictions* Student Book, for homework.

For Further Reflection

Answer will vary. Sample response.

They divide people in age groups because different aged people watch and prefer different types of programs. By dividing the population in age groups and taking a sample from each age group, they are sure to get reliable information for all age groups.

Section Focus

In this section, students evaluate results from surveys, samples, or experiments to determine whether or not there is a connection between apparently unrelated events. For example: *Is there a connection between where people live and how they vote? Does a new brand of insect repellent work and does it work better in some regions than in others? Does an orangutan in a zoo prefer blocks of a particular shape and color?* Students use tree diagrams, two-way tables, and chance trees to decide whether two events are independent or dependent.

Pacing and Planning

Day 5: Opinion Poll		Student pages 12–15
INTRODUCTION	Problem 1	Investigate the results of an opinion poll.
CLASSWORK	Problems 2–6	Use two-way tables and tree diagrams to compare opinion poll data from different parts of town and introduce dependent and independent events.

Day 6: Insect Repellent		Student pages 16–18
INTRODUCTION	Problem 7	Reason about experimental design.
CLASSWORK	Problems 8–12	Study the results of scientific experiments presented in two-way tables.
HOMEWORK	Problems 13 and 14	Reason about the chances of correctly guessing the type of block Koko, the orangutan, will pick.

Day 7: Glasses		Student pages 19–23
INTRODUCTION	Review homework.	Review homework from Day 6.
CLASSWORK	Problems 15–18	Investigate if there is a connection between gender and wearing glasses using a chance tree and a two-way table.
HOMEWORK	Check Your Work	Use (contingency) tables to analyze the results of various experiments and surveys.

Day 8: Summary		
INTRODUCTION	Review homework.	Review homework from Day 7.
ASSESSMENT	Quiz 1	Assesses Section A and B Goals
HOMEWORK	For Further Reflection	Explain the requirements for two events to be independent.

Additional Resources: Additional Practice, Section B, Student Book page 51

Materials

Student Resources
No resources required

Teachers Resources
No resources required

Student Materials
No materials required

* See Hints and Comments for optional materials.

Learning Lines

Dependent and Independent Events

An opinion poll about building a bridge across a river introduces the concepts of dependent and independent events. Students organize the data into a two-way table and a tree diagram to decide whether there is a connection between where a person lives and how a person votes.

Dependent and independent events were informally studied in the unit *Second Chance*; these concepts are revisited and formalized in this section. Some of the contexts, like wearing glasses from the unit *Second Chance*, are revisited in this section, and the issue of dependency is formalized. Students are made aware of the fact that although using models such as tree diagrams, two-way tables, and chance trees can support decisions about whether two events are dependent, these models cannot show why a connection exists or what type of connection exists between the variables studied.

Models

Students use tree diagrams, chance trees, and tables to organize information and make inferences about whether events seem to be dependent or not.

These models were used in previous units in the Data Analysis and Probability strand. The chance tree that was introduced and used in the unit *Second Chance* is now expanded: in addition to chances (now written as percents), the absolute numbers are now added to the tree.

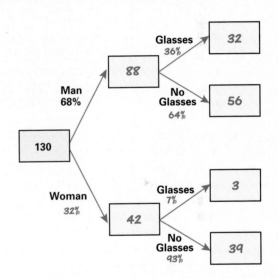

This information makes it easier to calculate expected value, which is explored in the next section.

At the End of This Section: Learning Outcomes

Students understand the difference between independent and dependent events. They can organize information in two-way tables, tree diagrams, or chance trees to decide whether events are dependent or independent. Students understand that if events are dependent, this does not tell why a connection exists. This relationship may be due to chance or to other unknown factors.

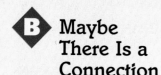
Notes

This page introduces the next context. Be sure that students understand that the results shown on the next page are a sample of the population. In addition, it is important to note that the location of the squares approximates the location of the respondent's house.

Maybe There Is a Connection

Opinion Poll

Next month, the citizens of Milo will vote on the following referendum.

Question: Should the city of Milo construct a second bridge between the east and west districts?

The local newspaper organized an opinion poll using a sample of the city's residents. The diagram on the next page shows the results. Each square represents a person who took part in the poll and shows approximately where he or she lives. A white square means that the person plans to vote "no," and a green square indicates that the person plans to vote "yes."

Reaching All Learners

Vocabulary Building

This would be a good opportunity to discuss referenda that have recently appeared on local election ballots. Make sure students understand that ballots often include more than electing people to office. A referendum will often "put before the voters" issues that would result in an increase in taxes, such as building a new school, maintaining roads, highways, parks, and so on.

Hints and Comments

Overview

Students are introduced to an opinion poll held in the town of Milo on the construction of a bridge. There are no problems on this page for students to solve.

About the Mathematics

In a survey, there may be a connection between two or more of the variables in the study. The same can happen in other situations were events are related. This section focuses on the concept of dependent and independent events. Students learn to evaluate results or outcomes to determine whether events that seem apparently unrelated are nonetheless dependent or not.

Planning

You may want to read the text on this page as a whole-class activity

B Maybe There Is a Connection

Notes

1a Students are likely to estimate by eye, but warn them to be careful. Because the shaded squares are darker, they may tend to overshadow the white squares.

2a Point out to students that the totals are given in the table, so they should be able to check their counts by comparing to the total.

2c It is important that students use good reasoning to support their answers. They should refer to the chart in support of their answers.

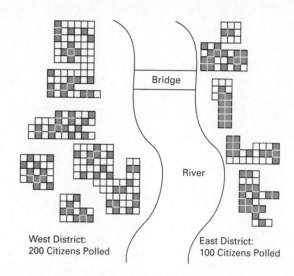

West District:
200 Citizens Polled

East District:
100 Citizens Polled

1. **a.** Do you think a majority of the citizens will vote for a new bridge? Make an estimate from the diagram to support your answer.

   b. Based on the sample, what is the chance that someone who lives in the west district will vote "yes"?

You might wonder whether there is a connection between where people live and how they plan to vote.

2. **a.** Count the actual responses to the bridge poll as shown in the diagram. Use a two-way table like the one shown to organize your numbers.

	West	East	Total
Yes			
No			
Total	200	100	300

   b. Which group of people, those in the east district or those in the west district, seem to be more in favor of the bridge?

   c. Do you think that there is a connection in the town of Milo between where people live and how they plan to vote? Explain your reasoning.

Assessment Pyramid

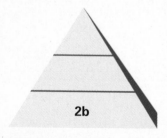

2b

Use two-way tables to find probability.

Reaching All Learners

Accommodation

Provide an enlarged copy of the diagram that students can mark on while they are making their counts. A copy of the table may be helpful as well.

Extension

Students could be asked to find the percent of yes and no votes for each group as well as the overall percentages.

Solutions and Samples

1. a. Answers will vary. The actual numbers are 135 yes to 165 no votes, so you might estimate that the majority will vote no.

b. 38.5%. There are a total of 200 squares on the west side, of which 77 are green. That means that of the sample of 200 people, 77 plan to vote yes. The chance a person on the west side would vote yes would be around $\frac{77}{200}$, or 38.5%.

2. a.

	West	East	Total
Yes	77	58	135
No	123	42	165
Total	200	100	300

b. Answers will vary. Sample response:

People in the east district seem to want the bridge more because 58 out of 100 people (more than half) voted in favor of the bridge. In the west district, only 77 out of 200 people (less than half) voted for the bridge.

c. Yes. A larger number of people on the west side want the bridge, but a larger percentage of those on the east side do. You can see that more than half of the people on the east side (58 out of 100) say they will vote yes, and fewer than half of the people on the west side (77 out of 200) will vote yes. Students may also calculate the percents.

Hints and Comments

Overview

Students investigate the results of an opinion poll in the town of Milo. The votes are represented by green and white squares on a diagram of the two districts of the town that were polled. They draw conclusions as to whether or not where people live is related to how they intend to vote. Students use two-way tables to organize information from the poll.

About the Mathematics

Information can be represented visually. Sometimes a visual model will represent the "story" of the data more clearly. In this case, the picture of the data conveys two variables: where a person lives and how the person votes. The ratio of the number of green squares (or the number of white squares) to the total is an estimate of the chance that the event connected with that type of square will occur. This way of finding probabilities is introduced in the unit *Take a Chance* and further formalized in the unit *Second Chance*. Students have also used this method earlier in this unit. Two-way tables are then used to organize the information on the two combined events; this makes it easier to calculate different ratios and chances. The concept of dependent and independent events and the way these influence chance was informally introduced in the unit *Second Chance* and is revisited and formalized in this section.

Planning

Students may work on problems 1 and 2 individually or in pairs. Discuss their answers as a whole class.

Comments About the Solutions

1. b. Here students must count the green and white squares to find the probability of a yes vote for someone in the west district. You might encourage them to share the counting, with one partner counting the total squares and the other counting the green squares. You may want to ask students whether, based on the answer for 1b, they think they should change their answers to 1a.

2. If students answered no, leave this until problem number 4, where this question is addressed again. You may want to discuss the difference between comparing absolute numbers and comparing ratios (relative comparison). This was introduced in the unit *Ratios and Rates* and used in the unit *Second Chance*.

B Maybe There Is a Connection

Notes

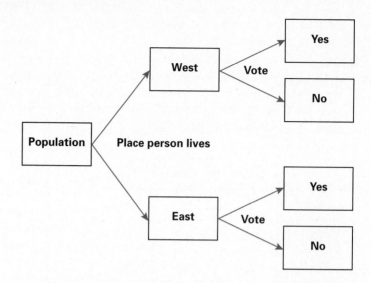

You can separate the 300 members of the sample into two groups: those who live in the west district and those who live in the east district. You can subdivide each of the two groups into two more groups: those who plan to vote "yes" and those who plan to vote "no," for a total of four groups. You can describe this situation using a tree diagram.

Because it is not possible to draw a branch for each person in the sample, branches are combined in such a way that you have two branches, one for the people living in the west district and one for the people in the east.

3 To solve this problem, students will need their answers from problem 2.

3b Be sure students understand that each of the boxes should contain a number: how many people fit that category.

3. **a.** What number of people does the branch for people living in the west district represent?

   b. Redraw the tree-diagram, filling in each of the boxes with the appropriate number from problem 2.

   c. Reflect Which method—a two-way table or a tree diagram—seems more helpful to you for finding out whether there is a connection between where people live and how they will vote? Give a reason for your choice.

Reaching All Learners

Accommodation

Blank copies of the tree for students to fill in may be useful.

Intervention

If students are having difficulty understanding the tree, choose a single square from the original diagram and help the students trace through the tree to see where that person would be counted.

Solutions and Samples

3. a. The branch or arrow represents 200 people.

b.

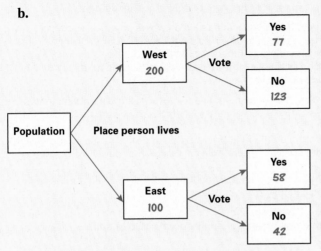

c. Answers will vary. For some students, the tree diagram may make the differences clearer, while other students may prefer the two-way table. The reasons students give will vary and can be very personal, for example:

- I find a table easier to read than a tree diagram.

- I find a table easier to draw than a tree diagram.

- A tree diagram more clearly shows the structure of the situation.

- I find it easier to calculate ratios from a two-way table.

Hints and Comments

Overview

Students use tree diagrams to represent the results of the opinion poll in Milo. They compare the two ways of describing the situation (two-way table and tree diagram).

About the Mathematics

This is a special version of a tree diagram. The use of tree diagrams to represent uncertainty is introduced and used in the units *Take a Chance* and *Second Chance*. On this page, the tree diagram is not yet a chance tree since only the absolute numbers are shown in the boxes. Chance trees were introduced in the unit *Second Chance*. In a chance tree, several branches may be combined into one, and chances are written with the branches; the tree diagram presented here shows the actual numbers and how these are divided over the several outcomes. Based on these numbers, chances can be calculated on each of the outcomes.

Note that the layout of this tree diagram is different from the layout of chance trees. The "titles" are now in the tree between the branches, whereas in chance trees, "the titles" are above the tree.

Planning

Students may work on problem 3 individually. Discuss the reasons they give in problem 3c.

B Maybe There Is a Connection

Notes

4 Students need to realize that, in this case, the numbers are different enough that there appears to be a connection. Some may note that it is possible that one of the samples was poor, but we need to assume that these are representative samples.

5 It is important that students are able not only to decide whether events are related but also to explain the connection, or suggest possible connections.

6a Some students may need to be reminded that the number polled on the east side is half the number polled on the west.

There are two possibilities for voting on the Milo bridge.

i. There is no connection between where people live and how they will vote. In other words, the two factors, or "events," are **independent**. Another way to think about this is that the chance of a "yes" vote is the same for all citizens, no matter on which side of the river they live.

ii. There is a connection. The two events are **dependent**. In this case, how a person votes is affected by where the person lives.

4. For voting on the Milo bridge, which possibility seems more likely to you, possibility i or ii? Give a reason for your choice.

If the events are dependent, sometimes you can explain the connection by looking carefully at the situation.

5. **Reflect** What are some reasons that people on different sides of the river might vote differently on the Milo bridge?

Now let's suppose there is no connection between where people live and how they will vote. In other words, those events are independent. In the first column of the two-way table below, you can see how people in the west district voted.

	West	East	Total
Yes	120		
No	80		
Total	200	100	300

6. a. Assuming that the events "where a person lives" and "how that person votes" are independent, how many people from the east district have voted "yes" and how many have voted "no"? Copy and complete the table. Explain how you got your answer.

b. **Reflect** In general, how can you use the numbers in a table or diagram to decide whether two events are dependent or independent? Hint: Use the word *ratio* or *percent* in your answer.

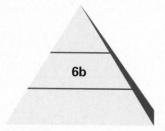

Assessment Pyramid

6b

Determine whether events are dependent or independent and find the probabilities.

Reaching All Learners

Vocabulary Building

Independent and *dependent* events are defined on this page. Independent events are two events that are unrelated, dependent events are events that are related.

Advanced Learners

Ask students to expand their answers to problem 6b to include a tree diagram for independent events and explain how it is clear that they are independent.

Intervention

If students have difficulty answering problem 6b, you might refer them to their answers to problems 3 and 6a.

Solutions and Samples

4. Option II: It is more likely that there is a connection. Explanations will vary. For an explanation, see also the answer to problem 2c. If the ratios or percents are quite different, it seems reasonable to investigate the possibility of a connection.

5. Answers will vary. Sample responses:

   People in the west district might vote differently from people in the east district if the places where most people work are in the west district; west district people live there and do not have to drive across the river. An airport and a train or bus station might all be located in one district. A large shopping mall might be located in one district. One district might be closer to a major highway

6. **a.** If the events were independent, 60 people of the east district should have voted yes and 40 should have voted No.

	West	East	Total
Yes	120	60	180
No	80	40	120
Total	200	100	300

   Explanations will vary. Sample explanation:

   In the west district, 120 out of 200 people voted yes, which is 60% voting yes and 40% voting no. If there is no relation, the ratios for yes and no votes must be the same in the east district.

   b. Explanations will vary. Sample explanation:

   In general, if the chance something may happen can be described for two samples by ratios or percents that are close to each other, there would seem to be no connection between the events. If the ratios or percents are quite different, it seems reasonable to investigate the possibility of a connection.

Hints and Comments

Overview

Students decide whether the events "where a person lives" and "how a person votes" are dependent. They think about reasons for a possible connection. They show what the outcomes could be for a situation where the events are not related in a two-way table.

About the Mathematics

The distinction between independent and dependent events is formally made here. Equal ratios (probabilities) imply that there is no connection and the two events are independent. Unequal ratios (probabilities) imply that there is a connection and the two events are dependent. If events are dependent, it is important to be able to find reasons for the connection.

Analyzing data may give reason to suppose a connection exists, but it cannot explain what causes the connection.

Planning

Students may work on problems 4–6 individually or in pairs. You may want to discuss students' answers in class.

Comments About the Solutions

4. Have students look back to their answer to problem 2c.

6. **a.** You may want to emphasize that this is a problem in which there is no connection. If there is no connection, it is reasonable to assume that the ratios would be about the same for both districts. It is important that all students realize this. Of course, the actual numbers will differ because of the different sizes of the populations.

B Maybe There Is a Connection

Notes

7 Experiments are designed with a control group to prevent people's beliefs and expectations from influencing the results. A control group is a set of people who receive no treatment.

8 Interpreting numbers in two-way tables can be difficult. This problem is intended to help students read the tables and extract and calculate with the important factors.

After problem 8, it may be helpful to have a conversation about what they notice about each of the four regions before proceeding with problem 9.

Insect Repellent

A new insect repellent was tested to see whether it prevents mosquito bites. It was not feasible to test the repellent on the entire U.S. population, so the researchers used a sample.

Because mosquitoes may be different in different parts of the country, the researchers ran the test in four different geographical regions. A sample of people was selected from each region and divided into two groups. Each person received a bottle of lotion. For one group, the lotion contained the new repellent, and for the other group, the lotion had no repellent. The people in each group did not know whether or not they received the repellent.

7. Why do you think the test was designed in such a complicated way?

The researchers ran the insect repellent test in four parts of the country and summarized the results.

Region I	R	NR	Totals
B	41	53	94
NB	79	27	106
Totals	120	80	200

Region II	R	NR	Totals
B	70	58	128
NB	40	32	72
Totals	110	90	200

KEY:
R = Repellent
NR = No Repellent
B = Bitten
NB = Not Bitten

Region III	R	NR	Totals
B	100	49	149
NB	30	21	51
Totals	130	70	200

Region IV	R	NR	Totals
B	50	61	111
NB	60	29	89
Totals	110	90	200

8. a. How many people were used for the sample from Region I?

b. In Region I, explain what the numbers 120, 41, and 79 represent.

c. What is the chance that a randomly selected person from the sample in Region 1 was bitten?

d. Would you change your answer to **c**, if you were told the person had used repellent?

9. If you knew people living in each of the four parts of the country, who would you encourage to use the repellent and who would you discourage? Explain your advice; use chance in your explanation.

Reaching All Learners

Intervention

Some students may need to be reminded that "chance" has a precise mathematical definition. The chance is the number of favorable outcomes divided by the number of possible outcomes.

If students have difficulty with problem 8, they can repeat the questions with the other regions. This would also provide students with some information that might make problem 9 more accessible.

Act It Out

Students could use four colored chips to show the four groups for a particular region. If each region were set up students would have a visual way to make a comparison in addition to the numerical.

Solutions and Samples

7. Answers will vary. Sample response:

The test was designed in such a complicated way so that it would be easy to determine whether the repellent really works. The group whose lotion contains repellent (the experimental group) can be compared to the group whose lotion does not contain repellent (the control group). It is important for people not to know which group they are in so that the results are unbiased. Sometimes people get better just because they think the medicine is supposed to make them better.

8. a. 200 people

b. 41 people received repellent and were bitten anyway, 79 people received repellent and were not bitten, and a total of 120 people were given the repellent.

c. 94 out of the 200 persons in Region I were bitten. The chance is $\frac{94}{200}$, or 47%.

d. Yes, the chance would change because now you only take into account the persons using repellent. So the chance a randomly selected person from Region I who uses repellent was bitten is $\frac{41}{120}$, or about 34%.

9. Explanations will vary. Sample explanation:

The repellent seemed to have the best effect in Region I. Fifty-three out of 80 people (about 66%) who did not use the repellent were bitten. However, only 41 out of 120 people (about 34%) who used the repellent were bitten.

The repellent also seemed to be effective in Region IV. So, one recommendation might be to use the repellent in Regions I and IV and to avoid using it in the other regions.

Region I: With repellent, about 34% were bitten; without repellent, about 66% were bitten.

Region II: With repellent, about 64% were bitten; without repellent, about 64% were bitten.

Region III: With repellent, about 77% were bitten; without repellent, about 70% were bitten.

Region IV: With repellent, about 45% were bitten; without repellent, about 68% were bitten.

Hints and Comments

Overview

Students study the results of a scientific experiment presented in four two-way tables.

About the Mathematics

Here, the context is changed from using a sample in a survey to using a sample in a scientific experiment. This type of experiment uses two groups, a control group and an experimental group. The data are presented in two-way tables. Students must interpret these data and draw conclusions. How chance can be found from information in two-way tables was introduced and used in the unit *Second Chance*. Students use this knowledge here. In these problems, students apply what they learned so far to a more complex situation.

Planning

Students may work on problems 7–9 in small groups. Be sure to discuss students' answers to problems 7 and 9.

Comments About the Solutions

9. Students must compare and interpret the data from the tables. If they have difficulty, you might discuss one of the regions in class. It is not necessary to calculate a percent for every cell in the tables. You can have students compare the tables more generally and at a glance. For example, students might make statements like the following: In Region I, about $\frac{1}{3}$ of the people who used repellent were bitten, whereas more than $\frac{1}{2}$ of the people who didn't use repellent were bitten. So using repellent seems to be effective in Region I.

For example, in Region II, more than half of the people were bitten whether they used repellent or not. In Region IV, about half of those who used repellent were not bitten, whereas $\frac{1}{3}$ who did not use repellent were not bitten.

Ape Shapes

Koko is an orangutan at the zoo. She is allowed to play with blocks that come in three shapes—cylinders, cubes, and pyramids. They also come in two colors—blue and orange. Here are 40 blocks that Koko took out of a bucket full of blocks.

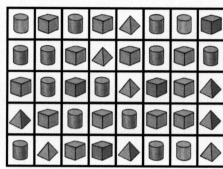

10 Students must realize that the chances can be found using ratios. Since probability is usually expressed using percents or decimals, the ratios must be converted.

11 Students need to organize the data in a two-way (cross) table. It may be helpful for students to begin by making tallies and then fill in the totals. Be sure to check students' counts before they move on since they need to have an accurate table for the next problems.

10. a. If Koko randomly chooses one of her 40 blocks, what is the chance that it will be a cube?

b. What is the chance that the block Koko chooses will be blue?

The zookeepers wonder whether there is a connection between the shape of a block and its color for the blocks Koko chose. In other words, does Koko like blue cubes better than orange ones? Orange cylinders better than blue ones? And so on.

The first step in answering this question is to organize the data.

	□	△	○	Total
Blue				
Orange				
Total				

11. a. Copy the two-way table and record the information about the 40 blocks Koko has chosen.

b. Is there a connection between block shape and color? How did you decide?

Reaching All Learners

Accommodation

It may be helpful to provide a tally chart for students to use in analyzing the 40 blocks.

Solutions and Samples

10. a. 16 out of 40 (or 40%)

   b. 20 out of 40 (or 50%)

11. a.

	☐	△	○	**Total**
Blue	4	4	12	20
Orange	12	5	3	20
Total	16	9	15	40

   b. Answers will vary. Sample response:

For cubes and cylinders, there seems to be a relation, for pyramids not. Koko seems to like orange cubes better than blue cubes ($\frac{12}{16} = 75\%$ of the cubes are orange), and she prefers blue cylinders ($\frac{12}{15} = 80\%$ are blue). She does not have a marked preference between the pyramids ($\frac{5}{9} = 55\%$ are orange).

Hints and Comments

Overview

Students investigate whether a connection exists between the color and the shape of the blocks selected by Koko, an orangutan at a zoo.

About the Mathematics

Students investigate again whether events are related. The information is presented visually. Students use a two-way table with three columns and two rows to organize and categorize the information. It may be easier to tally the information first. The situation is rather "abstract," which also implies there are no other factors in the situation to consider than the color and the shape of the blocks.

Planning

Students may work on problems 10 and 11 in pairs.

Comments About the Solutions

11. Students will need an accurate table to solve problems 12–14 on the next page.

B Maybe There Is a Connection

Notes

Koko and the zookeeper play a game with some zoo visitors. Koko picks up one of her 40 blocks and shows it to the visitors. The zookeeper, who is blindfolded, guesses the color.

The zookeeper guesses orange.

12. What is the chance that she is right?

During the game, one of the zoo visitors says that the shape Koko chose is a cube.

Again, the zookeeper guesses orange.

13. What is the chance that she is right this time?

13 This problem informally introduces students to the concept of conditional probability. Be sure students recognize that the denominator here is not all of the blocks, but only the cubes. Students should contrast this problem with problem 12.

The information that the shape is a cube changes the situation because now there are fewer possible blocks; in other words, it changes the chance that the block is orange.

14. What shape can Koko choose that will give the zookeeper the least help in guessing the color? Explain.

14 In this problem, students are asked to analyze the entire situation to consider all of the combined probabilities.

Glasses

In this two-way table, you see data on people wearing glasses. The data are from a sample of 130 people.

	Men	Women	Total
Glasses	32	3	35
No Glasses	56	39	95
Total	88	42	130

Assessment Pyramid

14

12, 13

Use different representations to describe probability. Make decisions using probability and expected values.

Reaching All Learners

Intervention

Students who are struggling with problem 14 could be asked to repeat problems 12 and 13 using different colors and shapes. This may help them in solidifying their understanding of the dependent nature of some situations and the independent nature of others.

Advanced Learners

Students could be challenged to come up with other sets of 40 blocks that show different dependencies, for example, a set where there is a connection between blue and sphere but no others.

Solutions and Samples

12. The chance is $\frac{20}{40} = \frac{1}{2}$, or 50%, because half of all the blocks are orange.

13. The chance is $\frac{12}{16} = \frac{3}{4}$, or 75%, because 12 of the 16 cubes are orange.

14. Giving the clue "pyramid" will provide the least help because there are about as many blue as orange pyramids Koko has chosen.

Hints and Comments

Overview

Students continue to investigate the situation of Koko selecting blocks. They reason about the chances of guessing correctly what type of block Koko picked. Next, students are introduced to the context of a relation between genders and the wearing of glasses.

About the Mathematics

Students informally reason about conditional probability. They have done so before in the unit *Second Chance*. Depending on the information students have, they will determine the probability of certain outcomes differently. If, for example, they know one of the characteristics of the blocks, they can use the information in the two-way table to find the chance it also has one of the other characteristics. For example, if they know a block is orange, it is more likely that this block is a cube than one of the other shapes. If no information was presented on the color, the chance a randomly chosen block is a cube is about the same as the chance it is a cylinder.

Planning

Students can work on problems 12–14 individually or in pairs.

Comments About the Solutions

14. Students must now reason the other way around. It is important that they can translate the situation as meaning that they need to find the shape for which the chance on each color is about equally likely. They need to reason from chance back to the data in the two-way table. This is a crucial problem to check whether students understand how conditional probability works.

Extension

You may want to have students draw a tree diagram for the situation on page 17 of the Student Book. There is no fixed order for the branches in the tree; either shape or color can go first. Note that the tree must have three branches for shape.

Notes

Before students begin this page, be sure they understand the two-way table on the previous page. You could ask students what they notice about the numbers in the table before they begin problem 15.

17 Students should notice that the chances in percents for every pair of lines in the tree add up to 100% (or to 1).

18 This problem is the key to the section. Students need to realize that if the chance is the same for glasses no matter the gender, then wearing glasses is independent. If, as in this case, the chances differ, the situation is dependent.

A person from this sample is chosen at random.

15. a. What is the chance that the person wears glasses?

    b. If you were told that the person is a woman, would you change your answer for part **a**? How?

The data from the table can be used to make a tree diagram.

16. Copy and complete the tree diagram by filling in the correct numbers in the boxes.

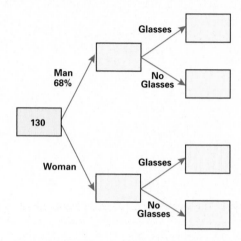

You can make the tree diagram into a **chance tree** by listing the chance, or probability, for each event. The chances are written next to the arrows. For example, the chance that a person from the sample is a man is 68%.

17. a. Explain how the 68% was calculated from the data in the table.

    b. Fill in the chance for each event in your tree diagram.

    c. Use the tree diagram to find the chance a randomly selected person from this sample is a man wearing glasses.

18. a. **Reflect** Explain how you can use the chance tree to conclude that wearing glasses is dependent on whether the person is a man or a woman.

    b. What would your chance tree look like if wearing glasses was independent of being a man or a woman?

Assessment Pyramid

Determine whether events are dependent or independent. Use chance trees to find probability.

Reaching All Learners

Intervention

Students who are struggling to understand what an independent tree would look like could be asked to create a two-way table where the situations are independent and then use that to make a chance tree.

Advanced Learners

Students could be asked to think of a situation in the school that they are not sure is independent or dependent. They could take a survey and create a chance tree to decide.

Solutions and Samples

15. a. The chance that the person wears glasses is
$\frac{35}{130} = 0.27$, or about 27%.

b. Yes. If the person is a woman, the chance she
wears glasses is $\frac{3}{42} = 0.071$, which is about 7%.

16.

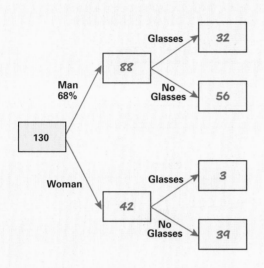

17. a. 68% was calculated by dividing 88 by 130.

b.

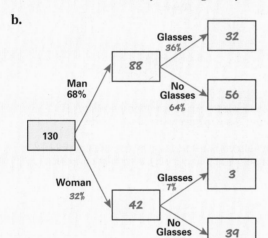

c. This chance is 32 out of 130, which is about 25%.

18. a. Answers will vary, Sample answer.

You can use a chance tree and compare the
chances for wearing glasses along the branches
for men and for women. For women, the chance
is 7%, and for men, this is 36%. This is very
different, so it would seem that a connection
exists and that the "events" might be dependent.

b. The tree would have the same percentages
of glasses and no glasses for both men and
women. For example, the percentage of the
women who wear glasses would be the same
as the percentage of men who wear glasses,
so they both would be 36%.

Hints and Comments

Overview

Students investigate if there is a connection between
gender and wearing glasses. They use a chance tree
and a two-way table to do so.

About the Mathematics

Students revisit a context they have seen in the unit
Second Chance. This problem context deals with
conditional probability, which occurs when two
events are dependent. For this particular context,
students will discover that "being male" and "wearing
glasses" are dependent. In such a case, the probability
of a person's wearing glasses changes according to the
gender of the person. Students do not need to know
the term conditional probability, or any formal rules.
They must realize the difference between finding the
chance of a combined event "men wearing glasses"
and finding a conditional probability: given that a
person is a man, what the chance he is wearing
glasses is. They find chances by using two-way tables,
tree diagrams, and chance trees and by reasoning.
The tree diagrams that were used to organize data are
now transformed into chance trees, as was done in
the unit *Second Chance*. Chances are written next to
the arrows that represent the events, now using
percents instead of fractions.

Planning

Students may work on problems 15–18 individually or
in pairs.

Comments About the Solutions

17. c. This is not an example of conditional probability,
it is a combined event. Students have to
determine the chance that someone from the
sample (of all the 130 people) is in the category
"men wearing glasses" (top-left cell of table).

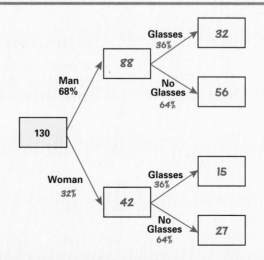

Notes

This page summarizes the section. At this point, students should be clear about the connection between the two-way table and the tree as well as understanding how to determine if the events are dependent or independent.

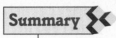

In this section, you studied methods to investigate whether two events are dependent or independent. Two-way tables, tree diagrams, and chance trees are three tools to help you make such decisions.

	Men	Women	Total
Glasses	32	3	35
No Glasses	56	39	95
Total	88	42	130

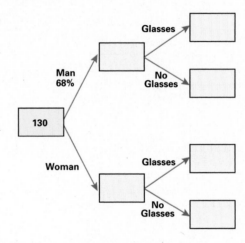

You can use each of these tools to decide whether members of particular groups are more likely to have a certain property.

While tools like this can help you decide if two events are possibly dependent, they cannot help you find out why a connection exists.

Reaching All Learners

Parent Involvement

Have students share the summary with their parents. They should show their parents where the numbers in the two-way table would be filled-in on the chance tree.

Hints and Comments

Overview

Students read the Summary, which reviews the main topics covered in this section.

Check Your Work

Garlic has been used in medicine for thousands of years by traditional healers. Recent studies suggest that garlic has many health benefits, such as lowering blood pressure.

The table shows results of a study with a sample of 200 people who evaluated whether garlic actually lowers blood pressure. Not all cells have been filled in.

	No Change in Blood Pressure	Lower Blood Pressure	Total
Using Garlic	27	73	
No Garlic			100
Total	87		

1a Be sure students understand that the information given is sufficient to fill in the entire table, there are no choices about what numbers to fill in where.

2 You may want to challenge some students to have the numbers of people who used garlic and those who didn't be different, but still have there be no connection.

1. **a.** Copy the table and fill in the missing numbers.

   b. What is the chance that a randomly chosen person in the study has a lower blood pressure?

   c. What is this chance if you were told the person had used garlic?

   d. Show how you can use the data in the table to make clear that a connection between using garlic and lower blood pressure might exist.

2. Make up numbers that show no connection between garlic and lower blood pressure. (Use a total of 200 people.)

Reaching All Learners

Study Skills

Before looking at the Summary, ask students to review Section B and write down what they think are the important ideas in the section. After discussing this in small groups, ask students to look at the Summary. What topics from the Summary were included on their lists? Does the Summary include items not on their lists? Do they have items that were not in the Summary? This strategy helps students review, helps them develop the ability to identify important ideas, ensures that they actually read the Summary, and helps them appreciate the value of the Summary section.

Solutions and Samples

Answers to Check Your Work

1. a.

	No Change in Blood Pressure	Lower Blood Pressure	Total
Using Garlic	27	73	100
No Garlic	60	40	100
Total	87	113	200

b. The chance that a randomly chosen person in the study has lower blood pressure is 113 out of 200, which is $\frac{113}{200} = 0.565$, or about 57%.

c. The chance would be 73 out of 100, or 73%. You only look at the 73 people of the 100 who used garlic.

d. The percentage of people with lower blood pressure is larger in the group that uses garlic; 73% of that group have lower blood pressure, while in the whole group, about 57% have lower blood pressure, and in the group that uses no garlic, only 40% have lower blood pressure. So there seems to be a connection. However, you cannot tell whether the garlic caused the lower blood pressure. And of course, the sample must be chosen carefully!

2. You can use different numbers in the table. One example is shown. If no connection exists, the percentage of people with lower blood pressure would probably be about the same in both the group that used garlic and the group that didn't use garlic.

	No Change in Blood Pressure	Lower Blood Pressure	Total
Using Garlic	49	51	100
No Garlic	52	48	100
Total	101	99	200

Hints and Comments

Overview

In Check Your Work, students assess themselves on the concepts and skills from this section. Students can check their answers on Student Book pages 56–58. They reflect on the topics addressed in this section in the For Further Reflection problem.

Planning

After students finish Section B, you may assign as homework appropriate activities from the Additional Practice section, located on Student Book page 51.

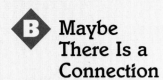

Some people have problems driving in the dark. Researchers wonder whether this is different for men and women.

3. **a.** Who would be interested in knowing whether there is a difference between men and women and driving in the dark?

Researchers have studied the ability to drive in the dark for a sample of 1,000 people, half of whom were women and half men. They found that 34% of the men and 58% of the women had problems driving in the dark. So they suspected that a connection exists.

b. Fill in the table with the correct numbers.

	No Problem Driving in the Dark	Problems Driving in the Dark	Total
Men			
Women			
Total			

3b It might be helpful to have students check their numbers with each other before they move on to part **c** to make sure they don't have any errors.

c. Make a chance tree that would represent the situation in the table.

d. What is the chance that a randomly chosen person from this group has problems driving in the dark?

e. Did you use the table or the chance tree to find the chance in part **d**? Give a reason for your choice.

4. At Tacoma Middle School, a survey was held to find how many hours a week students spend at home on their school work. These are the results.

4 Be sure students look carefully at the table before moving on to answer the problems on the next page. It is important that they understand the situation before they try to answer the argument presented.

	Less Than 3 Hours a Week	3 Hours a Week or More	Total
Grade 6	40	40	80
Grade 7	30	45	75
Grade 8	20	40	60
Total	90	125	

Assessment Pyramid

3ae

3bcd

Assesses Section B Goals

Reaching All Learners

Accommodation

It might be helpful to provide blank chance trees for some students for problem 3c so they do not spend too much time actually drawing the tree.

Advanced Learners

Students could be asked to expand on their response to problem 3d to show how each of the three representations could be used to find an answer.

Solutions and Samples

3. a. Possible answer:
The people in the traffic department might want to know because of safety reasons; eye doctors might be interested and try to prescribe glasses that will help; insurance companies might be interested for assigning insurance rates.

b.

	No Problem Driving in the Dark	Problems Driving in the Dark	Total
Men	330 (500 − 170)	170 (0.34 × 500)	500
Women	210 (500 − 290)	290 (0.58 × 500)	500
Total	540 (330 + 210)	460 (170 + 290)	1,000

First you fill in the column with the totals. Then you use the percentages to fill in the column for "problems driving in the dark." With the numbers from the last two columns, you can find the numbers in the first column for men and women. The totals can be found by adding up the numbers for men and women.

c. A chance tree:

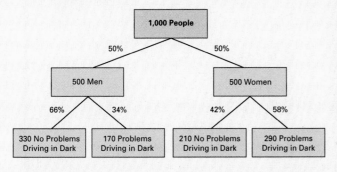

d. The chance that a randomly chosen person has problems driving in the dark is 460 out of 1,000, which is 46%

e. Be sure to tell which method you used to find your answer and give a reason like maybe the table is easier to read. You might not like the chance tree because all of the chances are figured out on the tree.

Overview

Students continue to complete the Check Your Work problems from this section. Students can check their answers on Student Book pages 56-58. They reflect on the topics addressed in this section in the For Further Reflection problem.

Planning

After students finish Section B, you may assign as homework appropriate activities from the Additional Practice section, located on Student Book page 51.

Notes

4 Encourage students to refer to the table and to make trees as appropriate to support their answers.

a. Julie states, "There is no connection between hours spent on school work at home and grade level, since in all grades about 40 students spend 3 hours a week or more." Do you agree with Julie? Why or why not?

b. Based on these results, do you think there is a connection between grade level and hours spent on school work at home? Explain your answer.

 For Further Reflection

Explain what it means for two events to be independent. Give an example different from the ones in this section to show what you mean.

Assessment Pyramid

4ab

☐ FFR

Assesses Section B Goals

Reaching All Learners

Parent Involvement

Have students share their work on the Further Reflection problem with their parents. The adults in their lives have other ideas about examples of situations not in the book that are independent or dependent.

Solutions and Samples

4. a. You might agree with Julie, but she is wrong. She is looking only at the numbers in the middle column. She should also take into account how many students are in each grade level and then compare the percentages. In grade 6, half (50%) of the students spend 3 hours a week or more, and in grade 8, 40 out of 60 or $\frac{2}{3}$ of the students spend 3 hours or more on homework.

b. Yes, there seems to be a connection. The higher the grade level, the more, likely a student is to spend 3 hours or more per week on homework, although the percents are pretty close for grades 7 and 8.

Grade 6: 40 out of 80 is 50%.

Grade 7: 45 out of 75 is 60%.

Grade 8: 40 out of 60 is 67%.

For Further Reflection

Answers will vary. Sample answer:

If two events are independent, it means that one event happening has nothing to do with the other event happening. There is no connection. If you were to talk about chances, you could say that for independent events the chance that the one event happens has nothing to do with the chance that the other event happens as well. An example of two independent events is: "going to school" and "the weather being sunny." These events are not related.

Hints and Comments

Overview

Students continue to complete the Check Your Work problems from this section. Students can check their answers on Student Book pages 56–58. They reflect on the topics addressed in this section in the For Further Reflection problem.

Planning

After students finish Section B, you may assign as homework appropriate activities from the Additional Practice section, located on Student Book page 51.

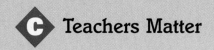

Section Focus

In this section students study the distribution of results from samples and compare this to the distribution in the population. They graph data in number-line plots and histograms. They compare data from several samples by comparing the plots and using statistical measures such as median and spread. They investigate what happens when samples get larger. They make chance statements based on data from samples and population.

Pacing and Planning

Day 9: Fish Farmer		Student pages 24 and 25
INTRODUCTION	Activity, page 24	Simulate the situation of catching fish from a pond.
CLASSWORK	Problems 1–4	Study combined sample (for the whole class) to draw conclusions about the lengths of two types of fish.
HOMEWORK	Problems 5 and 6	Use the results of the simulation to estimate the size of two types of fish.

Day 10: Fish Farmer (Continued)		Student pages 26 and 27
INTRODUCTION	Review homework.	Review homework from Day 9.
CLASSWORK	Problems 7–9	Study the distributions of the length of fish from the pond and compare this to the distribution in samples.
HOMEWORK	Problem 10	Draw conclusions based on data gathered from a simulation.

Day 11: Backpack Weight		Student pages 28–31
INTRODUCTION	Problem 11	Investigate data on the weight of students' backpacks.
CLASSWORK	Problems 12 and 13	Use medians and spread to compare backpack data.
HOMEWORK	Check Your Work For Further Reflection	Student self-assessment: Make conclusions based on the analysis of data from various problem contexts.

Additional Resources: Additional Practice, Section C, Student Book pages 51–53

Materials

Student Resources

Quantities listed are per student.

- **Student Activity Sheets 2** and **3**

Teachers Resources

Quantities listed are per class.

- At least 200 fish data cards

Student Materials

No materials required

* See Hints and Comments for optional materials.

Learning Lines

Sample and Population

In this section, the relation between samples and the population is further explored. Students simulate catching fish from a pond to determine the average length for different types of fish. Students experience that small samples can have much variability. Recording the results of growing samples, for example, by combining the results of all the samples taken by the whole class helps students realize that variability can be reduced as the sample size increases. A larger sample is also more likely to be representative of the population. The data from the samples (that is, the type of fish and its length) are graphed in number-line plots and histograms. Students were introduced to these types of graphs in the units *Picturing Numbers* and *Dealing with Data*.

Students notice that as the sample gets larger the distribution of the lengths of the two types of fish is more distinct. They use the sample data to verify claims made about the lengths of the two types of fish. Later they check this against the population data and conclude how well the sample data reflect the data of the population.

Graphs and Chances

In the unit *Second Chance*, students used data presented in graphs, like histograms, to estimate chances. They interpreted the relative frequency of an outcome as the experimental (empirical) chance for that outcome. This connection between data analysis and probability is further explored in this section.

Instead of calculating the relative frequencies from a histogram, students may also estimate chances by looking at the distribution of the outcomes to make more general statements about chance.

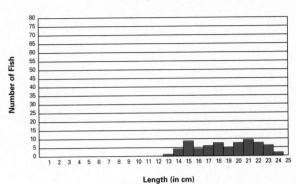

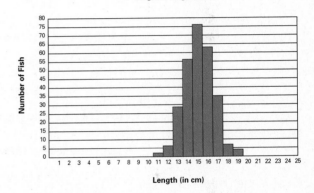

Students may, for example, conclude that the chance for several lengths of GE fish is about the same chance for all lengths of fish in the upper graph above. In the lower graph, the chance of catching a fish of about 16 cm is much greater than the chance of catching a fish that is 19 cm.

Students compare distributions of data for backpack weight for several samples of students from different grades. These data are graphed in number line plots; students use the median and the spread to describe the distributions.

At the End of This Section: Learning Outcomes

Students understand how to describe the distribution of data and make statements about experimental chance based on relative frequencies of certain outcomes. They improve their understanding of the relationship between a sample and a population by studying the effect of a growing sample.

Reasoning from Samples

Fish Farmer

A fish farmer raises a new species of fish he calls GE. He claims that these fish are twice as long as his original fish. One year after releasing a bunch of original fish and a smaller amount of the GE fish into a pond, students were allowed to catch some fish to check his claim. You are going to simulate this situation.

 Activity

Your teacher has a set of data cards. Each card represents a fish from the pond.

The cards with the word *original* on them represent the original fish; the cards with *GE* on them represent the GE fish. On each data card, you see the length of a fish.

Every student in your class "catches" five "fish" from the "pond."

1. a. Explain how catching the "fish" in the activity is taking random samples.

  b. Record the lengths of the 30 fish that were caught by you and five other students from your class, keeping track of whether the lengths belong to the original fish or the GE fish.

  c. On **Student Activity Sheet 2**, make two different plots of the lengths: one for the original fish and one for the GE fish.

1a Be sure that students see you shake the cards in a container and/or that they are allowed to pick any five cards they want so that they see that the cards they have are a random sample of all the cards.

Reaching All Learners

Accommodation

It may be helpful to provide a chart or table for students to use to collect the data on the lengths of the 30 fish so that they have one list for "regular" and one for "GE."

You can make the groups smaller and have students make graphs of fewer data. About 20 data points is the minimum.

Extension with Technology

Instead of doing the activity this way by drawing data cards, a statistics computer program, like for example Tinkerplots, may be used to simulate the situation of taking samples of fish from the pond and graphing the data.

Solutions and Samples

1. a. Explanations will vary. Sample explanation:

Each card represents one fish in the pond. The cards are taken from the box without looking; they are well mixed, so each card has an equal chance of being picked. So the five cards a student picks are a random sample taken from the population of all data cards (all fish).

b. Graphs will vary depending on the samples of students. Sample student graph, of 20 data points

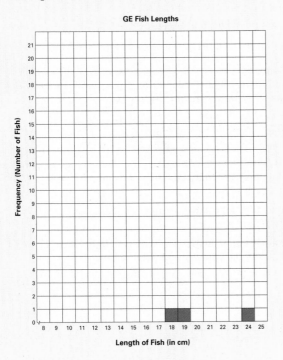

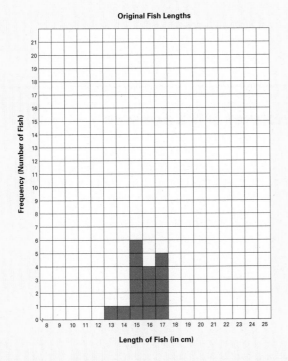

Hints and Comments

Materials

Student Activity Sheet 2;
at least 200 data cards with fish data (Note: A set of data cards should have been sent with the Teacher's Guide). If you do not have a set of data cards, you can create these from the template pages found in the back of this book. Instead of copying and cutting these out, you may want to use small index cards and write the data of one of the fish on each of them.

Overview

Students simulate the situation of catching fish from a pond; they record whether their fish are "original" fish or of a special type, so-called GE fish. And they record the length. They graph their data.

About the Mathematics

A situation can sometimes be simulated to get information that is hard to get in reality. Simulations can be used, for example, to find out how likely certain outcomes are in complex situations. To design a simulation, information must be available about the characteristics of the population that will be studied. In this section, students simulate catching samples of two types of fish from a pond. By taking samples, they investigate whether length and type of fish are connected.

There are two ways of taking samples: sampling with replacement and sampling without replacement. Here sampling without replacement is used because the samples of all students are combined to "grow" a bigger sample. If the population is large enough, the difference between sampling with and without replacement will hardly make a difference on the outcomes.

Planning

The Activity is part of a whole class-activity. Students can work on problem 1a individually, but problem 1b must be done in small groups. Problems on pages 24–27 represent one problem context.

Comments About the Activity

Put the data cards into a box or paper bag and have each student draw five cards and record the type of fish (GE or original) and the corresponding length. After each drawing, shake to mix the remaining cards, and have the next student draw five of the data cards.

1. b. Students may want to make a number-line plot, a bar graph, or a histogram. Have each student first plot his or her own data; next have every student in the group sum up his or her data—the type of fish and its length—while the other students in the group add the data to their own graphs.

Notes

Throughout this page, students are asked to make claims and then to justify them. Be sure that there is some consensus within the class about what "counts" as a justification.

4 If it is possible, it might be helpful to copy each smaller group's list of data for each of the other groups so that they have the information they need to do this problem. The information could also be recorded on the board or on chart papers.

4 and 5 You may want to have a transparency of **Student Activity Sheet 2** available, so that class results can be shared on the overhead projector.

2. a. Write at least two observations about the lengths of the two types of fish based on the plots you made with your group. One observation should be about the mean length of the fish.

   b. Compare your observations with the observations of another group. What do you notice?

The fish farmer claimed that GE fish grew twice the size of the original fish.

3. Based on your data about the length of fish in the plots, do you agree or disagree with the fish farmer's claim about the length of the GE fish? Support your answer.

Add all the data points from every student in your class to the plots.

4. Now would you change your answer to problem 3?

5. What claim could you make about the lengths of the GE fish compared to the original fish based on the graphs of the whole class data? How would you justify your claim?

The fish farmer only wants to sell fish that are 17 centimeters (cm) or longer.

6. a. Based on the results of the simulation activity from your class, estimate the chance that a randomly caught GE fish is 17 cm or longer.

   b. Estimate the chance that a randomly caught original fish is 17 cm or longer.

   c. Estimate the chance that a randomly caught fish is 17 cm or longer. How did you arrive at your estimate?

Assessment Pyramid

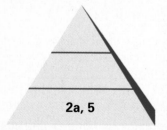

2a, 5

Use graphs and measures of central tendency to describe data.

Reaching All Learners

Accommodation

For some students, it may be less time consuming for them to use some technology, (Excel, Tinkerplots, graphing calculator) to make the graph.

Intervention

For problem 6, it is helpful to organize the data in a two-way table to find the chances. You may want to point this out to students.

Solutions and Samples

2. a. Sample observations:

- There are many more original fish than GE fish.
- Some GE fish are much longer than all original fish.
- The lengths of the GE fish have a larger range.
- The original fish are typically around 15 or 16 cm long. This will be the mean.

b. Answers will vary since this depends on the observations of the other groups. The samples will probably vary quite a lot since they are small. However, it could well be that each group has a mean of about 15-17 cm for the original fish. The mean of the GE can vary a lot between groups since the sample size is very small.

3. Disagree. Explanations will vary, depending on students plots. Sample answer:

The original fish have a mean of about 15 cm, but the GE fish do not have a mean length of about 30 cm.

4. This depends on the samples, but the plots should still show that while the GE fish are bigger; then are not really twice as big. Sample answer:

GE fish are larger; over half of the GE fish that were caught were over 21 cm long, but the typical original fish that was caught was about 15 to 17 cm long, which is not half as much as the GE fish

5. Answer will vary based on the graphs. Sample graphs of the entire class data, based on a sample of 100 fish.

Sample answers:

- All of the larger fish that were caught were GE fish.
- The GE fish seem to be in general around 21 cm long, while the original fish are around 15 cm. So the GE fish are about one and a half times as long as the original fish.
- On average, the original fish are about 15.5 cm long, and the GE fish about 19.3 cm long. So a better estimate of the ratio would have been 3 to 4 instead of 1 to 2.
- Some GE fish are very long (up to almost 25 cm) and twice the size of some original fish (about 12 cm). However, overall they are certainly not twice the size of the original fish.

Hints and Comments

Materials
Student Activity Sheet 2 (one per student);

See more Hints and Comments on page 92.

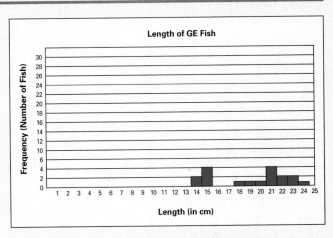

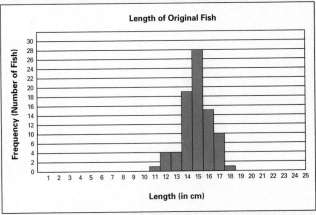

6. a. Answers will vary, depending on students' samples. Sample answer based on a sample of 100 fish from the whole population:

	Up to 17 cm	17 cm or Longer	Total
Original	71	11	82
GE	6	12	18
Total	77	23	100

Based on the data in the table, the chance that a randomly caught GE fish is longer than 17 cm is $\frac{12}{18}$, or $\frac{2}{3}$, which is about 0.67, or 67%.

b. The chance of catching an original fish longer than 17 cm is $\frac{11}{82}$, which is about 0.13, or 13%.

c. The chance that a randomly caught fish is longer than 17 cm is $\frac{23}{100}$, which is about 0.23, or 23%.

C Reasoning from Samples

Notes

Be sure students understand that these are histograms, so taller bars represent more fish of that length.

It would be helpful to have both graphs on overheads so that everyone is looking at the same graph and they can be overlapped as a way to compare.

The fish farmer caught 343 fish from the pond and recorded the lengths. He graphed the lengths and made these histograms. The graphs are also on **Student Activity Sheet 3**.

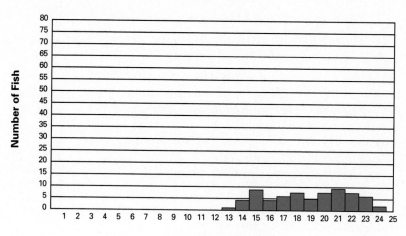

Length of GE Fish

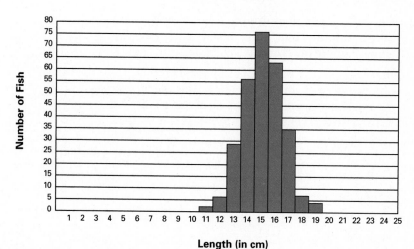

Length of Original Fish

Reaching All Learners

Accommodation

If you have students who have difficulty reading graphs and the values for each of the bars, prepare in advance a table of values to use with the questions about these two histograms.

Hints and Comments

Materials

Student Activity Sheet 3 (one per student)

Overview

Students study the graphs of the lengths of all 343 fish in the pond. There are no problems on this page for students to solve. The problems with these graphs are on Student Book page 27.

◆ Reasoning from Samples

Notes

8a In order to answer the problem, students must combine the data. Some may do it visually, but some may want to draw the data from the GE fish onto the graph of the original fish so that they can see the entire population.

9 This problem requires students to grapple with sample size in two different ways. Be sure students are clear about what the differences are between the two answers they are comparing.

10 Students should see that, once they have the numbers, it is much easier to make the necessary comparisons.

---

7. a. If you caught an original fish at random, what length (roughly) is most likely? Use the data in the histograms and give reasons for your answer.

b. If you caught a GE fish, what length would be most likely?

Remember: The fish farmer only wants to sell fish that are 17 cm or longer.

8. a. Based on the information in these graphs, estimate the chance that a randomly caught original fish will be 17 cm or longer.

b. Estimate the chance that a randomly caught GE fish will be 17 cm or longer.

c. Estimate the chance of randomly catching a fish that is 17 cm or longer.

9. a. Compare your answers to problems 6 and 8. Are they similar? If they are very different, what might explain the difference?

b. Why is the answer to 8c closer to the answer to 8a than to the answer for 8b?

You can use a two-way table to organize the lengths of the fish that were caught.

	Up to 17 cm	17 cm or Longer	Total
Original			
GE			
Total			343

10. a. Copy the two-way table into your notebook and fill in the correct numbers using the data from the histograms for the total of 343 fish. You already have a few of those numbers.

b. What is the chance the fish farmer will catch a GE fish?

c. **Reflect** How can you calculate in an easy way the chance that he will catch an original fish?

d. What is the chance that he catches an original fish that is 17 cm or longer?

e. Which type of fish do you advise the fish farmer to raise? Be sure to give good reasons for your advice.

Assessment Pyramid

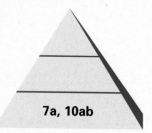

7a, 10ab

Use graphs and measures of central tendency to describe data.

Reaching All Learners

Intervention

If students are having difficulty with problem 8, have them draw a line on the graph to show which fish are big enough.

For problem 8c, make sure students understand that they need to combine data from both graphs since the problems are about all fish.

Solutions and Samples

7. a. Answers will vary. Sample answer.

- Most likely it would be between 15 and 16 cm because this is the mode. There are 76 of these fish.

- Most likely the length is between 15 and 18 cm because most data (a cluster of data) are in the middle.

b. Answers will vary. Sample answer.

- It is hard to tell because there is not really one length that is most common. The lengths are between 14 and 23 cm.

- Although not that many GE fish were caught, it seems that given the sample, a typical length for GE fish would be between 20 and 21 cm.

- Most likely it is around 20 cm but it can be plus or minus 5 cm.

8. a. Estimations will vary. Sample estimation:

- The chance that an original fish caught is larger than 17 cm is about one sixth. This can be found by fitting the bars.

- Based on the information in this graph the chance can be calculated, the chance is $\frac{46}{277}$, which is about 0.17 or 17%.

b. Estimations will vary. Sample estimation:

- The chance that a GE fish caught is larger than 17 cm is about 75%.

- The chance can be calculated and is $\frac{49}{66}$, which is about 0.74 or 74%.

c. Answer will vary. Sample estimation:

- About 25%, I kind of added the graphs together into one histogram and eyeballed the part of the bars above 17 cm.

- The chance can be calculated: If you catch a fish at random, the chance that it is longer than 17 cm is (46 + 49) ÷ (277 + 66), which is about 0.28 or 28%.

9. a. Answers will vary, this depends on the actual samples. Sample answer:

- The differences are not very large: 67% versus 74% for GE fish, 13% versus 17% for original fish, and 23% versus 28% for the whole population.

b. This answer to 8c is closer to the answer to question 8a than to 8b because the group of original fish is much larger than the group of GE fish. The original fish population has a bigger influence on the overall chance of catching a fish larger than 17 cm than the smaller GE population. One way to think about this is to imagine a population with only 1 GE fish and 9 original fish.

Hints and Comments

Materials

Student Activity Sheet 3

Overview

Students study the distributions of the lengths of all original and all GE fish from the pond. They compare these distributions to those from their samples. They draw conclusions based on the data.

See more Hints and Comments on page 93.

Most samples of size two would reflect the nine original fish, and the one GE fish would not have much influence on the overall results.

10. a.

	Up to 17 cm	17 cm or Longer	Total
Original	231	46	277
GE	17	49	66
Total	248	95	343

b. The chance that the fish farmer will catch a GE fish is $\frac{66}{343}$, which is about 0.19, or 19%.

c. The chance that he catches an original fish is about 81%. This can be found as the complementary chance of the chance found in part **a**, it is 100% − 19%.

d. The chance that he catches an original fish longer than 17 cm is $\frac{46}{343}$, which is about 0.13, or 13%. Note that in this case, 46 has to be divided by the total number of 343.

e. Answers will vary. Sample advice to the fish farmer:

- He should grow GE fish because they are generally larger. And from the data in the table, you can see that the chance a GE fish is larger than 17 cm is bigger (74%) than the chance that an original fish is that long (13%).
  Of course, you cannot know if there are other factors that would influence his decision. Perhaps GE fish are harder to grow since now there are not many in his pond. Or these GE fish may not be typical of all GE fish.

Notes

11 This problem is a good opportunity to be sure all of your students have an efficient way to calculate 15% of a number.

11b Encourage students to pick reasonable weights for students. You may need to remind them that to convert from pounds to kilograms, you divide by 2.2.

12 Make sure students realize that the percentages (backpack weight of body weight) are graphed and not the weights themselves.

Backpack Weight

Too much weight in backpacks can cause shoulder pain or lower-back pain. Doctors say that you should not carry more than 15% of your own weight.

11. a. Randy weighs 40 kilograms. What weight can he carry based on the doctors' rule?

   b. Choose two other weights for students and calculate the maximum backpack weight for these weights.

Scientists decided to check the amount of weight students at an elementary school carry in their backpacks.

The scientists made a number line plot of the weights carried by a sample of students from grades 1 and 3.

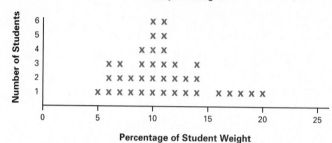

Backpack Weights

12. a. What do you think they concluded from this data set?

   b. **Reflect** Based on the data from this sample, would it be sensible to conclude that most students at the elementary school do not carry too much weight in their backpacks? Give reasons to support your answer.

Assessment Pyramid

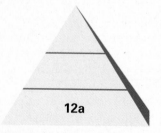

12a

Use graphs and measures of central tendency to describe data.

Reaching All Learners

Act it Out

Students could be asked to find out what percent of their own body weight their backpack is. If you do this in class, it is important to have students weigh themselves and their own backpacks so that there is no public knowledge of another's weight.

Solutions and Samples

11. a. According to the rule, Randy can carry 15% of 40 kg, which is 6 kg. Strategies may vary. Sample strategy:

10% of 40 kg is 4 kg, and 5% of 40 kg is half of this, so this is 2 kg. So 15% of 40 kg is 4 + 2 = 6 kg.

b. Answers will vary depending on the weights students choose. Student results should be 15% of the selected weight.

12. a. Answers may vary. Sample answer:

They probably concluded that there is not much reason to worry. The mean is just above 10%, and there are only a few students, 5 out of 38, carrying too much weight.

b. Answers will vary. Sample answers:

- If the sample is taken randomly, a conclusion may be that the weight percentages in grades 1 and 3 at that elementary school are mostly within the 15% limit. This could be different at another school, and for older students (next question), and even on another day.

- Since only students from grades 1 and 3 were in the sample, you cannot draw conclusions for all students at the elementary school.

Hints and Comments

Overview

Students investigate data on the weight of backpacks of students. Based on different samples, they decide whether they can conclude that these are too heavy or not, according to a rule.

About the Mathematics

There is a difference between concluding that a rule works for individual cases or for a group. For example, the rule that backpack weight should be no more then 15% of your own weight can be checked by each individual. But if someone wants to investigate whether the backpacks of elementary school students are too heavy or not, they will take a sample and study the distribution. In this case, data on the weight of the students and the backpacks in the sample are collected. These data are not graphed directly. First a calculation is made to find the percentage that the backpack weight is of the students' weight. These data are then graphed. Students investigate this situation and reflect on the way samples are taken and data are presented.

Planning

Students can work on problems 11 and 12 in small groups. Discuss the answers to 12b in class.

Comments About the Solutions

11. b. Students can choose the weights themselves. Some students may choose weights they find easy to use in the calculations, while others may want to be realistic and use weights of people they know, still other students may use numbers to show they can make more difficult calculations as well. You may discuss students' work in class.

12. b. You may want to discuss the fact that the sample is only taken from grades 1 and 3, so it is not representative of all elementary school children, and the fact that it is taken at one elementary school. Students may also indicate that it is important to know more about the five students with backpacks that are too heavy.

Reasoning from Samples

Notes

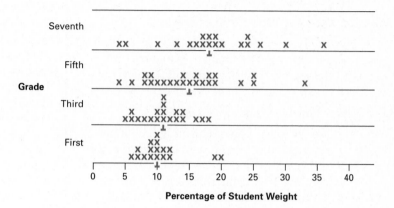

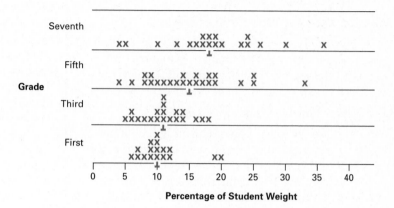

13 In this problem, students should use what they have learned about statistics to make conclusions about the different grades. You may want to ask students, *Why was the median indicated and not the mean? Would the mean be helpful in this case?* (Most likely not, because of the extreme values.)

The scientists wondered whether older students carried more weight in their backpacks. They decided to collect data on students in some of the upper grades as well.

Here are all their data from the sample of students in grades 1, 3, 5, and 7.

The red markers represent the medians of the group from each grade.

Backpacks

13. a. How would you characterize the differences in medians between grades 1, 3, 5, and 7?

   b. What does the median of a group tell you?

   c. How does the spread of the percents compare for the four grades? What does this mean about the weight students in each sample carried in their backpacks?

   d. What might you conclude about the amount of weight students carry in their backpacks? Support your ideas with arguments.

Reaching All Learners

Extension

Students could be challenged to make up the graph that they would expect for grade 9 students.

Solutions and Samples

13. a. The median weight percentage is larger as students get older, although the difference between grades 1 and 3 is probably not significant.

b. The median is the middle value or the mean of the two middle values of a data set. Half of the data points are left and half of them right of the median. The median is therefore in the center of the data points when they are ordered and is one way to describe the group as a whole.

c. Answers may vary. Sample answer:

- The spread in percentages is the largest for grade 7. It gets smaller for lower grades, but the spread for grades 1 and 3 is almost equal. It means the weights students carry with respect to their body weight varies a lot in grade 7 and less in grades 1 and 3.

- For grade 1: percentages range from 5% to 20%

- For grade 3: from 4% till 19%

- For grade 5: from 3% till 32%

- For grade 7: from 3% till 37%

- The spread for grades 5 and 7 is almost the same and is much larger than that for grades 1 and 3. The spread for these two grades is almost equal.

d. Answers will vary. Sample answer:

In grades 1 and 3, most students do not carry too much weight. However, in grades 5 and 7 many students do carry more than they should, especially in grade 7. In grade 5, the mean is just above 15%, and in grade 7, the mean is around 18.5%. One reason could be that they have more homework in the upper grades.

Hints and Comments

Overview

Students continue their investigation on the data on backpack weight. They use medians and spread to compare the data.

About the Mathematics

Data from samples can be graphed on number-line plots. The distributions of the data can then be studied and compared. It is important to use both a measure of center (like median or mean) and a measure of spread to compare distributions. In the example on this page, students use median and an informal idea of spread. The number line plots may be viewed as pre-versions of box plots. Box plots and the median were introduced and used in the unit *Dealing with Data* and were also used in the unit *Insights into Data*.

Planning

Students may work on problem 13 in small groups; you may want to discuss their arguments for part **d.** in class.

Comments About the Solutions

13. You may remind students to the measures of center and spread they have seen in the previous units *Dealing with Data* and *Insights into Data*.

d. You may want to discuss with students what these data tell and what you don't know about the samples studied. For example, data points at 10% for grades 1 and 7 both indicate that a student's backpack weighs 10% of the student's body weight. But the actual weights of students and backpacks for these data points will be different. You may have students make up underlying data (backpack weight and students weight) for some of the data points.

Reasoning from samples

Notes

Be sure students read the Summary, and it might be helpful to call on students to point out the important ideas presented.

 Reasoning from Samples

Summary

Small samples from the same population can be very different. Because small samples can have so much variability, it is important that a sample is large enough to get a sense of the distribution in the population.

It is also important that the sample is randomly chosen.

Based on data, you can estimate chances of particular events.

- For example, what is the chance of randomly catching a fish that is 17 cm or longer? What is the chance that it is smaller than 17 cm?

- If the chance that a randomly caught fish is 17 cm or longer is 23%, then the chance of catching a fish with length up to 17 cm is $1 - 0.23 = 0.77$, or in percentages: $100\% - 23\% = 77\%$. We say that these chances **complement** each other.

If you draw a conclusion from a sample, you have to be careful about how the sample was taken and from what population.

- For example, if you just study grades 1 and 3 students and their backpacks and find that their backpacks are not too heavy, you cannot make any conclusions about the backpack weights for students in general.

Check Your Work

The police have set up a sign that shows drivers how fast they are driving. Students at the Bora Middle School are still worried about speeding cars near the school. Using the speed sign, they decide to write down how fast cars go during the hour before school.

Reaching All Learners

Accommodation

This summary is very text heavy. It might be helpful to provide a copy for weak readers to highlight or take notes on in another way.

Parent Involvement

Have students share the summary and their work on the "Check Your Work" Section.

Vocabulary Building

Students might think of complementary probabilities as a pair of chances that add up to 100%.

Hints and Comments

Overview

Students read the Summary, which reviews the main topics covered in this section. In Check Your Work, students will assess themselves on the concepts and skills from this section.

Planning

After students finish Section C, you may assign as homework appropriate activities from the Additional Practice section, located on Student Book pages 51–53.

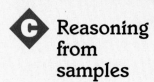
Notes

1 Have students share their lists so that they gain a broader view of the advantages and disadvantages.

These are the data values one student collected (in miles per hour):

24 28 27 26 31

And those of another student: 26 17 22 27 25

And of a third student: 25 27 28 32 32

1. Comment on the difference in the three sets of data they collected.

Here is the complete data set of speeds the students collected (in miles per hour).

			Speed (mi/hr)			
24	32	29	29	28	17	26
28	28	28	29	24	22	28
27	25	25	29	31	27	32
26	30	23	22	27	24	32
31	30	32	30	26	25	27
18	29	21	21	32	28	24
24	22	19	27	28	32	26
26	30	30	33	25	26	27
25	36	23	25	26	27	19

2 This problem is intended to once again have students think about the problems with small samples.

2. Make a plot of these values. Then use the plot and any statistics you would like to calculate to write a paragraph for the school officials describing the speed of the traffic on the road before school.

3. List some advantages and disadvantages of large samples.

 For Further Reflection

Does using a graph of the data help you understand how to estimate the chance of an event? Explain why or why not.

Reaching All Learners

Extension

If students concluded in problem 2 that speeding was not a problem, ask, *How many more data over the speed limit they would have to add for them to conclude that speeding was a problem?*

Solutions and Samples

Answers to Check Your Work

1. The samples are very small and give very different impressions of how fast the cars are going. In the first and third samples, four out of five cars drive faster than 25 mi/h, but in the second sample, only two do so. The second sample does not give much reason to worry about speeding cars, but the other two samples are more alarming.

   One similarity is that the median in all three is around 27 mi/h.

2. Your paragraph can have different plots and descriptions. You can make a histogram, a number-line plot, a box plot, or any other graph that you think will work. The examples below show a number-line plot and a histogram. The red marker represents the median.

   Be sure that you use the numbers to tell a story about speeding.

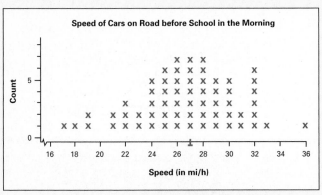

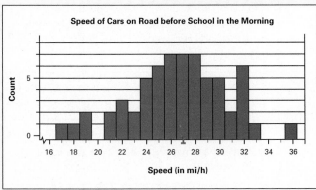

Here are some examples.

- I think that speeding is a problem. The dot plot of a sample of the speeds of 63 cars as they go past the school in the morning shows that over half of the cars are going as fast or faster than 27 mi/h, which is speeding. Most of the speeds were right around the speed limit between 24 and 28 mi/h, but about two thirds of them were going faster than the 25 mi/h speed limit. Four cars were going less than 20 mi/h, but one was 11 mi/h over the limit.

Hints and Comments

Overview

Students complete the Check Your Work problems from this section. Students can check their answers on Student Book pages 59–61. They reflect on the topics addressed in this section in the For Further Reflection problem.

Planning

After students finish Section C, you may assign as homework appropriate activities from the Additional Practice section, located on Student Book pages 51–53.

- I do not think speeding is a problem. Half of the cars were going just a little bit over the 25 mi/h speed limit. You can tell from the plot that just a few cars were going faster than 30 mi/h, and only one car was really speeding at 36 mi/h. Most of the rest, about 75% of them, were within 5 miles of the speed limit, which shows that they were really not going too fast.

3. An advantage of large samples, provided they are randomly selected, is that you can get a fairly good estimate of the center and spread of the distribution. A disadvantage of large samples is that they can be expensive and time-consuming to conduct. You might think of other advantages and disadvantages.

For Further Reflection

Sample answers:

- A graph of data may help estimate the chance of an event because, for example, in a histogram you can "eyeball" what part of the bars is at or above or below a certain value, and you can use this as an estimate for the chance of this outcome.

- A graph of data may help to estimate chances only a little because it is hard to visually estimate chances since they are fractions. It is easier to use the numbers, like the relative frequencies of certain outcomes.

Section Focus

The concept of expected value is formalized in this section. Students calculate, for example, the expected revenue for several toll options, the expected number of readers that will become customers, and the expected score for a basketball player. Students use chance trees to model situations and compute probabilities. They relate chance and expected value.

Pacing and Planning

Day 12: Carpooling		Student pages 32–34
INTRODUCTION	Problem 1	Calculate the money collected for a toll road given the toll per motorist and the number of cars.
CLASSWORK	Problems 2–7	Use chance trees to represent the survey results for drivers that plan to use the toll road's regular or new carpool lanes and to predict the money collected (expected value) under this new toll plan.
HOMEWORK	Problem 8	Predict the money collected under this new toll plan if different survey results are used in the calculations.

Day 13: Advertising		Student pages 34–36
INTRODUCTION	Problem 9	Use a chance tree to represent the number of newspaper readers who will read an advertisement and then become customers.
CLASSWORK	Problems 10–12	Use chance trees and tables to determine expected values.
HOMEWORK	Problems 13 and 14	Study a table containing data about the life span of mayflies and use the data to calculate the mayfly's life span.

Day 14: Free Throws		Student pages 36–39
INTRODUCTION	Review homework.	Review homework from Day 13.
CLASSWORK	Problems 15–18	Use a tree diagram with probabilities (chance tree) to represent data in a two-way table.
HOMEWORK	Check Your Work	Student self-assessment: Determine the chance for various events using chance trees.

Day 15: Summary		Student page 39
INTRODUCTION	Review homework.	Review homework from Day 14.
ASSESSMENT	Quiz 2	Assesses Section C and D Goals
HOMEWORK	For Further Reflection	Describe the concept of expected value to another family member.

Additional Resources: Additional Practice, Section D, Student Book pages 53 and 54

Materials

Student Resources

No resources required

Teachers Resources

No resources required

Student Materials

No materials required

* See Hints and Comments for optional materials.

Learning Lines

Expected Value

The concept of expected value, informally addressed in the unit *Second Chance*, is now formalized in this section. Chance trees, which were introduced in the unit *Second Chance* — as a special type of tree diagram — and were used in previous sections of this unit, are now used to explore and calculate expected values. To make the computation of expected value easier to understand, "absolute" numbers are added to the chance trees, as in the example shown.

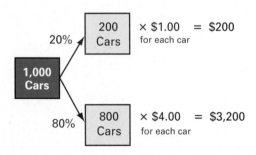

The total expected amount of tolls is found using the chance tree. The average expected value can be found by dividing the total of tolls collected, which is $3,400, over the 1,000 cars. This results in an expected toll of $3.40 per car. The average expected value can also be calculated by multiplying an outcome by its chance and adding the results for the several outcomes. In the example of the toll road, this would be 0.2 × $1.00 + 0.8 × $4.00 = $3.40 per car. This method is not explicitly addressed in this section. Students explore what happens if they start with a different number of cars, and they discover that the expected value only depends on the chances of the different outcomes. Expected value and mean are related when students calculate the expected life span of mayflies.

Models

Students use the chance tree with absolute numbers to calculate expected values. This chance tree was introduced in Section B in this unit. Students also use data presented in tables to calculate expected value. To do so, they must first reorganize the information.

At the End of This Section: Learning Outcomes

Students understand the meaning of expected value and can calculate and use it to make decisions. They use chance trees with absolute numbers to calculate expected value. They can also calculate expected value from data in a table. Students informally connect expected value to the (mathematical) mean.

Notes

You might want to introduce this section with a conversation about highway congestion and why carpools might help. Students who completed the unit *Ratios and Rates* have examined this idea before.

1 and 2 Both of these problems involve simple numeric calculations and provide a chance to see if your students are comfortable with the calculations.

Expectations

Carpooling

On one toll road in the city, each motorist pays a toll of $2.50. One day, the Department of Transportation counted 1,400 cars that used the toll road between 8:00 A.M. and 9:00 A.M.

1. During this time period, how much money was collected?

The Department of Transportation wants people to carpool in order to reduce traffic on the toll road. The Department is considering creating a "carpool only" lane for cars with three or more people. The toll for cars in the carpool lane would be reduced to $1.00. At the same time, the toll for cars in the regular lanes would be raised to $4.00.

The Department of Transportation takes a survey and estimates that when the regulation goes into effect, 20% of the cars will use the carpool lane.

2. If you see 100 cars enter the toll road, how many would you expect to use the carpool lane?

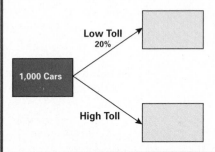

From the survey, the department also believes that on a typical morning between 8:00 A.M. and 9:00 A.M., the number of cars using the toll road will decrease from 1,400 to 1,000 due to the carpooling efforts.

3. Copy and complete the chance tree that displays the expected traffic after the change.

Reaching All Learners

English Language Learners

Be sure students understand what a toll road is as well as what a carpool is.

Extension

Have students write all the possible ways to pay the $2.50 toll. Students should think of a systematic way to find all possible combinations of dollar bills and coins.

Solutions and Samples

1. $3,500 ($2.50 × 1,400 = $3,500)

2. You would expect about 20 cars to use the carpool lane (20% of 100).

3.

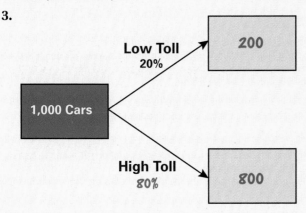

Hints and Comments

Overview

This section introduces students to the notion of expected value. On this page, students familiarize themselves with the context of a toll road. They investigate the effect of a proposed car pool lane in a toll road situation by completing a chance tree to determine how many cars are expected to use which lane.

About the Mathematics

The expected value is the same as the mathematical mean. Students learned how to calculate the mean in the unit *Dealing with Data*. A chance tree is a graphic representation of a problem situation in which all relevant information is pictured. Students have used chance trees in the unit *Second Chance*, however, in that unit no absolute numbers were written in the chance tree. Writing the absolute numbers is done here to make calculating the expected value more easy.

In this situation, as in many others students have seen so far, statistics and chances are more meaningful for a large group than for an individual. The fact that one car has a 0.20 chance of paying a low toll actually means that, on average, one out of every five cars pays the low toll or that for a large group of cars, $\frac{1}{5}$ will pay the low toll. For an individual car, the 0.20 chance of paying a low toll is not meaningful information.

Planning

Students may work on problems 1–3 in small groups. Students used tree diagrams and chance trees in the units *Take a Chance* and *Second Chance*, and in the previous sections of this unit.

Comments About the Solutions

2. Students can represent the chance in a number of different ways: 20% is the same as $\frac{1}{5}$, 0.2, or 1 out of 5. They can choose the way that makes calculating easy for them.

Notes

4 This problem begins the introduction of expected value. If students have difficulty, have them use their diagram from problem 3 to help them determine how many cars will pay each of the tolls.

4. a. How much money does the Department of Transportation expect to collect between 8:00 A.M. and 9:00 A.M.?

   b. What will be the average toll charge per car during this hour?

The department also wants to know how many people use the toll road. To answer this question, some assumptions were made: A car that uses the carpool lane has three occupants, and a car in one of the regular lanes has only one occupant.

5. Using those assumptions, how many people will travel on the toll road from 8:00 A.M. to 9:00 A.M. on a typical morning?

The Department of Transportation is trying to decide whether to carry out the carpooling plan. It considers the change in the amount of toll money collected, the change in the number of cars on the road, and several other factors.

6. Do you think the department should carry out the carpooling plan? Justify your answer.

In solving the carpool problem, you used a process that can be represented as follows:

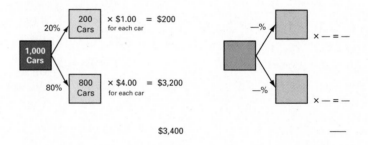

7 This problem can be done as a whole-class activity. You might ask students to explain what each part of the diagram represents. It is critical that students understand this problem before continuing with the next because this problem combines all the calculations that students have used to this point.

The diagram on the right is a general version of the one on the left.

7. Explain the process shown in the diagrams.

Solutions and Samples

4. a. $3,400

Sample strategy:

200 cars × $1.00 = $200

800 cars × $4.00 = $3,200

$200 + $3,200 = $3,400

b. The average toll charge per car will be $3.40 ($3,400 ÷ 1,000 = $3.40).

5. 1,400 people

Sample strategy:

200 cars × 3 = 600 carpool users

800 cars × 1 = 800 non- carpool users

600 + 800 = 1,400 travelers

6. Answers will vary. Sample answers:

- Yes, the department should make the change because the 1,000 cars will hold 1,400 people (see answer to problem 5) and, before the car-pool lane, most likely everyone of the 1,400 people traveled in his or her own car. So there will be 400 fewer cars on the road, which will lessen pollution, reduce road wear and tear, and be safer.

- No, the department should not make the change. It will lose money. For the 1,400 cars with one person, they got $3,500 in tolls. For the 1,000 cars that have the same 1,400 people, they will only collect $3,400. So the department will lose money ($100) with the new plan.

7. Explanations will vary. Sample explanation:

The cars are divided according to the lane they use, and the percents indicate the percentage that is expected to use each lane or the chance a car will use that lane. The toll for all the cars in each lane can be calculated. Then, all the tolls are added to find the total amount of toll revenue.

Hints and Comments

Overview

Students continue solving problems in the context of the toll road. They determine how much money is expected to be collected and how many people are expected to travel on the toll road using the proposed plan. Students explain how to use a diagram to solve a problem about expected value.

About the Mathematics

By using absolute numbers of cars, the expected total toll can be calculated. The expected value is the average toll per car (the mathematical mean). This value does not depend on the number of cars. It can be calculated by multiplying the value of each possible outcome (in this case, each toll fare) by its chance. Students, however, will use the absolute number of cars on this to find the total toll expected, they will then divide the total toll by the number of cars to find the expected value. The chance tree with the absolute numbers helps students use this method. The notion of expected value is introduced here, but the term *expected value* is not yet introduced. This is done on the next page, student book page 34.

Planning

Students may work on problems 4–6 in small groups. Discuss students' solutions and strategies for problem 4, before they proceed with the other problems. Problem 7 can be done as a whole-class activity.

Comments About the Solutions

4. You may want to discuss with students if they would find another average toll if another number of cars was used instead of 1,000.

6. Try to have students use several factors in their reasoning. You may have students write their answers to problem 6 in their journals. You may want to discuss their argumentations in class.

7. The total is in the box on the left, while the two branches (arrows) show how the total is split. The meaning of each outcome and its chance are expressed as a fraction, percent, or decimal and is written with the branch. The boxes at the ends of the branches show the resulting (expected) numbers for each outcome. The chances in fractions, percents, or decimals should always add up to one (or 100%).

Notes

Be sure students understand the previous page before moving to problem 8. In this problem, students are asked to repeat the process with different numbers.

Students need to extract the important details from the context introduction on this page in order to complete the problems on the next page.

The amount $3,400 represents what you expect to happen; in this case, it is the amount of money you expect to collect. Mathematicians call this an **expected value**. Sometimes it is useful to calculate the expected value as a rate. In this example, the rate would be the expected toll charge per car.

Kathryn works for the Department of Transportation. She has looked at a different survey and thinks that 30% of the cars will use the carpool lane.

8. a. Using Kathryn's results, make a tree diagram representing the toll money collected for 1,000 cars.

b. How much money does Kathryn expect the department to collect between 8:00 A.M. and 9:00 A.M.?

c. Under Kathryn's plan, what is the expected value, that is, the average amount that a car on the toll road would pay?

d. Reflect Who would be interested in this value and why?

Advertising

Ms. Lindsay is about to open a new store for teens. To reach her potential customers, she decides to advertise in the local paper. There are about 15,000 teens who read the paper. This is her "target group."

Ms. Lindsay knows that not every teenage reader will read her advertisement. She also realizes that not every reader of the advertisement will become a customer. She estimates that 40% of the readers of the paper will read the ad. Also, she expects only 10% of those who read the ad to become customers.

Assessment Pyramid

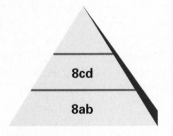

8cd

8ab

Make decisions using probability and expected values. Use tree diagrams and different representations to describe probability.

Reaching All Learners

Vocabulary Building

The term *expected value* is introduced on this page. The expected value is the value that is predicted using the assumed probabilities. Be sure students realize that the expected value in a situation is based on probabilities, so it is not exactly what one should expect to earn.

Extension

You may want to have students make a diagram to represent a similar toll road situation in which there is a higher or lower percentage of cars using the carpool lane or a different number of total cars using the toll road.

Solutions and Samples

8. a.

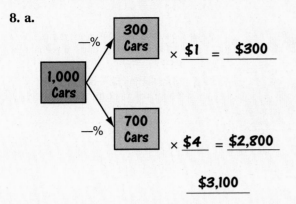

$$300 \times \$1 = \$300$$

$$700 \times \$4 = \$2,800$$

$$\$3,100$$

b. $3,100. Strategies will vary. Sample strategy:

300 × $1.00 = $300

700 × $4.00 = $2,800

$300 + $2,800 = $3,100

c. The average amount is $3.10 per car ($3,100 ÷ 1,000 = $3.10).

d. The highway department might be interested because they could use this value to estimate the total revenue for different time periods.

Hints and Comments

Overview

Students are introduced to the term expected value and calculate the expected value of tolls on the toll road if more cars use the carpool lane. They are introduced to a new problem situation involving advertising.

About the Mathematics

While the mean is used as a statistic for a situation in which all data are known, the expected value is used in a situation in which the population is not known, and samples are taken. From the samples, the chance on each outcome can be estimated. These chances can be used to find the expected value, which is in fact a theoretical estimation for the mean of the total population (which is unknown). Students do not need to know this background. They can calculate the expected value in the same way as they calculate the mathematical mean. They learned to do this in the unit *Dealing with Data*.

Planning

You may want to read the text about expected value with the whole class. Students may work on problem 8 individually or in pairs.

Comments About the Solutions

8. Students who understand how to calculate expected value may not want to draw a tree diagram. Ask them to write out their calculations instead.

Notes

9a Students should realize that the second step in the diagram shows 10% and 90% of the 6,000 ad readers, *not* 10% and 90% of the total 15,000 readers.

9b This problem is challenging. If students have difficulty, you might ask, *How many customers are there out of how many readers?* (600 out of 15,000) This answer, 4%, means that 4% of the teens who read the paper are likely to become customers. At this point you can ask, *What is another way you could arrive at the answer of 4%?* [10% of 40% is 4%] It is not critical for all students to see this relationship at this point.

10 This problem is similar to 9, but the tree is more complicated.

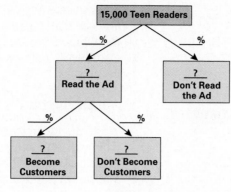

9. a. Copy the diagram and complete it to show the percent of teens in each category.

b. What is the chance that a teen reader will become a customer?

Another way to get more customers is to run the ad on two consecutive days. The chance that a teen reader will see an ad on the first day is 40%, and the chance that a teen reader will see an ad on the second day is also 40%. In this situation, the chance tree looks like this.

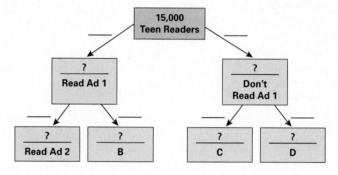

10. a. Copy the chance tree into your notebook and fill in the chance for each of these events.

b. What are the meanings of boxes B, C, and D?

c. After two days of advertising, how many members of the target group can be expected to have read the ad?

d. What is the chance that a member of the target group will become a customer?

11. Reflect What other things would you need to know in order to advise Ms. Lindsay about whether to run the ad twice?

Reaching All Learners

Hands-on Learning

It might be helpful for some students to set up the situation in problem 9 using counters. If you start with 150 counters the numbers work out the same, but there is less counting.

Accommodation

Copies of blank trees will be helpful for some students.

Extension

You may want to have students extend the chance tree to show what it will look like if the ad is run three times. You could also have students draw chance trees for other percents or other numbers of readers.

Solutions and Samples

9. a.

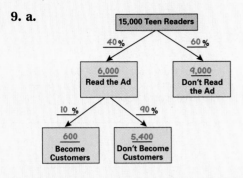

b. The chance that a teen reader will become a customer is $\frac{600}{15,000}$, or 4%.

10. a.

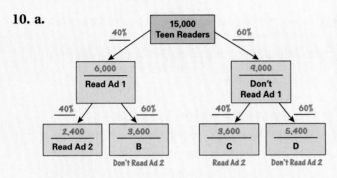

b. Box **B** represents people who read ad 1 but did not read ad 2. Box **C** represents people who read ad 2 but did not read ad 1. Box **D** represents people who did not read any ad.

c. The number of people expected to have read the ad after two days is 9,600. This is the sum of the totals of boxes **A**, **B**, and **C** (2,400 + 3,600 + 3,600), or all people minus the total of box **D** (15,000 − 5,400).

d. 6.4%. Strategies may vary. Sample strategies:

- Ten percent of the 9,600 people who read the ad are expected to become customers, this is 960 customers; The chance of a reader becoming a customer thus is $\frac{960}{15,000} = 0.064 = 6.4\%$.

- Students may also solve this problem by adding a row to the chance tree, calculating 10% of boxes **A**, **B**, and **C**, and then adding those numbers (although this is more tedious then the first method described) and use the ratio of the number of customers to all readers to find the chance.

11. Answers will vary. Sample response:

If Ms. Lindsay runs the ad twice, she is expected to get more customers: 960 instead of 600. She could also consider, however, the costs of advertising. The effect of rerunning the ad decreases over time.

Hints and Comments

Overview

Students investigate a diagram representing the situation involving advertising that was introduced on Student Book page 34. They explore the number of customers that an ad is expected to generate.

About the Mathematics

The situation studied on this page is similar to the situation about tolls, but more complex since it is about combined events: two events that are dependent. Students can use chance trees to model the situation. In this situation, chances and expected value are explicitly connected through the use of chance trees that have absolute numbers in them as well. Students used chance trees for combined events in the unit *Second Chance*. They can use either the multiplication rule for chances (introduced and used in the unit *Second Chance*) or the ratios of the absolute numbers in the trees to find the chances on the different outcomes. Students have not yet multiplied chances that were expressed as percentages. You may want to pay explicit attention to how this should be done by converting the percentages into decimals or fractions first.

Planning

Students may work on problem 9 and 10 in small groups. After students finish problem 10, you may want to discuss problems 9 and 10 and how to use chance trees. Students may work on problem 11 individually.

Comments About the Problems

9. b. Students might use a ratio table to convert the ratio into a percent as follows:

Customers	600	6	12	4
Readers	15,000	150	300	100

D Expectations

Notes

Expected Life of a Mayfly

For a science project, a group of students hatched 1,000 mayflies and carefully observed them. After six hours, all of the mayflies were alive, but then 150 died in the next hour.

Hours	6	7	8	9	10	11	12
Number Still Alive	1,000	850	600	250	100	20	0

12. Based on the data in the table, write two statements about the life span of mayflies.

13 a. Based on these data, what is the chance that a mayfly lives 8 hours or more?

   b. Use the students' data to determine the expected life span of a randomly chosen mayfly. Explain how you found your answer.

13b There are several ways to approach finding the answer to this problem. Encourage students to think about how many mayflies live for a certain amount of time. They can then use this information to think about the expected value.

Think about how long people live.

14. a. **Reflect** Why would an expected value be useful?

   b. How could sampling affect the expected value?

Free Throws

Mark is on a basketball team. He is a very good free-throw shooter with an average of 70%. This means that on average he will make 70% of the free throws he takes. You can also say that his chance of making a free throw is 70%.

15. If Mark takes 50 free throws, how many of these do you expect he will miss?

Assessment Pyramid

14ab

Reason about likely and unlikely samples and factors that can bias a survey. Make decisions using probability and expected values.

Reaching All Learners

Intervention

Some students may need more direction in a way to find the expected life span of mayflies. These students could start by thinking about the probability that a fly would live 6 hours [100%], then 7 hours and so on.

Extension

Students could find the free-throw percentage for different players in the WNBA or the NBA.

Solutions and Samples

12. Statements will vary. Sample statements:

- All mayflies live between 6 and 12 hours.
- More then half of the mayflies are still alive after 8 hours, after 9 hours only a quarter is alive.

13. a. 600 out of 1,000 mayflies are alive after 8 hours, which is 60%. So the chance a mayfly in this sample lives 8 hours or more is 60%, or 0.6.

b. Answers and explanations will vary.

- Some students may suggest that the mean can be used to find the life span. This is the most time-consuming method.

Hours	6	7	8	9	10	11	12
Number Still Alive	1,000	850	600	250	100	20	0

− 150   − 250   − 350   − 150   − 80   − 20

150 flies lived between 6 and 7 hours; 250 flies lived between 7 and 8 hours; 350 flies lived between 8 and 9 hours; 150 flies lived between 9 and 10 hours; 80 flies lived between 10 and 11 hours; and 20 flies lived between 11 and 12 hours.

Using the midpoint of each interval, the average might be calculated as follows:

$(150 \times 6.5) + (250 \times 7.5) + (350 \times 8.5) + (150 \times 9.5) + (80 \times 10.5) + (20 \times 11.5) =$ 8,320 hours for 1,000 flies, or an average life span of about 8.3 hours.

- A second method is to use a median value. The expected life span will then be about 8.5 hours, since about half of the mayflies live at least that long.

- A third method (although less accurate) involves reasoning more globally about the situation. After 6 hours, mayflies start to die and after 12 hours they are all dead, so the expected life span lies about halfway between 6 and 12 hours. So, the expected life span is about 9 hours.

14. a. Answers will vary. Sample response:

An expected value for people's life spans gives some idea of how long a person will live. For example, a man born in the United States in 2001 is expected to live around 74 years; a woman is expected to live around 80 years. This information is useful for the government as it makes plans for social security, for health care providers, or for insurance companies that offer life insurance policies.

Hints and Comments

Overview

Students study a table containing data about the life span of mayflies. They use the data to calculate the expected life span of a mayfly. Next they are introduced to a situation of free throws, based on the chances they calculated expected scores.

About the Mathematics

Expected life span is an example of an expected value. In the context on this page, it is the mean of the hours the flies live. Students learned how to calculate the mean in the units *Picturing Numbers* and *Dealing with Date*. Expected life span can also be interpreted in a more informal way. It can then be estimated using more informal methods (see the Solutions and Samples column). In this case, the mean cannot be calculated directly from the data in the table since these are cumulated data.

Planning

Students may work on problems 12–14 individually or in pairs. You may want to discuss the answers to 13b and 14 in class. Students can work on problem 15 individually.

Comments About the Problems

12. If students have difficulty interpreting the numbers in the table, you may want to ask them where the 150 flies mentioned in the text above the table can be found in the table.

14. You may want to discuss that expected life span in general does not tell much about people's individual life expectancies. It is, in fact, the expected life span at the time of birth. Insurance companies use statistics to determine one's life expectancy based (among other things) on the person's current age. You may want to have students think of ways to collect data to find the expected life span. More information on life expectancy can be found on the Internet, for example on: http://www.cdc.gov/nchs/fastats/lifexpec.htm

b. Answers will vary. Sample response:

If you calculate expected life span using a small group of people from only one region of the country or any other biased sample, you may get a poor estimate.

15. Mark is expected to miss 30% of 50 shots, which is 15 free throws.

Notes

16b Be sure students realize that there are two different ways to score one point.

17 It can help to add a row for score points to each of the boxes in the bottom row. Note that one shot made is counted as one point.

18 Note that the tree has only a second set of branches if the first shot is made. Otherwise the player will not get a second free throw. The tree is not symmetrical. Still per event in the tree, all percents or chances with the branches must add up to 100% or to 1.

Basketball games have different free-throw shooting situations. In a one-and-one situation, a player can take the second free throw shot only if the player made the first one. In the two-point free-throw situation, the player can take two free throws regardless of whether the first shot is made.

Mark is often in the two-point free throw situation. This means that he can take two shots. Suppose during a series of games, he will be in 100 two-point free-throw situations.

16. **a.** Copy the chance tree for Mark in the two-point free-throw situation and complete it.

   b. In how many of the 100 times Mark takes two-point free throws do you expect he will score one point?

   c. What is the chance that Mark will score two points in a two-point free-throw situation?

17. **a.** Use the chance tree to calculate how many points Mark is expected to score in 100 two-point free-throw situations.

   b. What is his expected score per two-point free-throw situation?

The other free throw situation is the one-and-one situation. A player can try one free throw. If the player makes this shot, the player gets to try a second one. If the player misses the first shot, no second one is allowed. In this situation, Mark still has a 70% free throw average.

18. **a.** Make a chance tree for Mark in a one-and-one free-throw situation. Suppose again that he was going to shoot 100 one-and-one free throws.

   b. What is the average score you expect Mark to make in a one-and-one free-throw situation? Show how you found your answer.

Assessment Pyramid

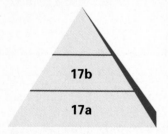

Make decisions using probability and expected values. Use chance trees to find probability.

Reaching All Learners

Extension

Have students figure out the expected points per two-point free-throw bonus attempt for a player with a different free-throw percentage and compare that to the expected points per free-throw attempt in a one-and-one situation.

Solutions and Samples

16. a.

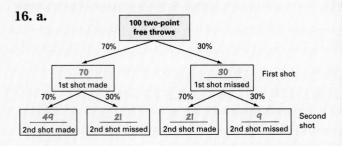

b. Mark scores one point if he misses one shot and makes one. This is the case in 21 + 21 = 42 situations out of 100.

c. The chance he scores two points is 49 out of 100 or 49%.

17. a. He is expected to score 2 points 49 times; 1 point 21 + 21 or 42 times; and 0 points 9 times. This is a total of 140 points in 100 shots.

b. His expected score is $\frac{140}{100}$ or 1.4 points.

18. a.

```
              100
          one-and-one
          free throws
        70%          30%
      /                  \
    70                    30
  1st shot made       1st shot missed
  70%    30%
  /        \
 49         21
2nd shot made  2nd shot missed
```

b. Now you expect Mark to score 2 points in 49 out of 100 cases, to score 1 point in 21 out of 100 cases, and to score 0 points in 30 out of 100 cases. So in 100 one-and-one bonus situations, you expect Mark to score a total of 49 × 2 + 21 = 119 points. So Mark's expected average score is 1.19 points.

Hints and Comments

Overview

Students investigate the expected scores for two free-throw situations in basketball for a player whose chance of scoring is known.

About the Mathematics

In the case of sports, statistics are often used to indicate how well players perform. A free-throw average of 70% means that a player is, on average, expected to score in 70% of free throws taken. His or her expected score can be said to be 0.7 per throw. Another way of expressing what the 70% means is saying that the chance a player scores on each throw is 70%. These different meanings of 70% are connected here. Chance trees are once again used to calculate chances on combined events as well as to calculate expected values.

Planning

Students may work on problems 16–18 individually or in pairs. You may want to have a class discussion first on the rules for basketball.

Comments About the Solutions

16. You may have students look back to the chance tree for problem 10 on Student Book page 35.

17. b. You may want to discuss with students what the expected score per free throw means. It is not an actual score the player can make each time. It is in fact a chance or an average over a larger number of situations; it can be used to predict expected scores or to compare the ability of different players.

Notes

Be sure that students are clear about how the chance tree is used to find the expected value.

Expectations

In this section, you investigated expected values.

To find the expected value of an event, you need to know the chance associated with the possible outcomes.

A chance tree shows the chance for each outcome. Note that chance can be expressed as a percent or as a fraction.

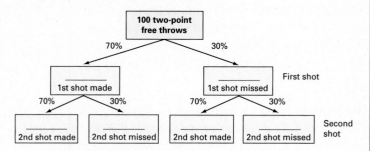

You can use a chance tree to find expected values.

Check Your Work

On a toll road around the city, 25% of the cars are expected to use the carpool lane. The toll is $3.00 for a car in the regular lanes and $1 per car in the carpool lane.

1. **a.** Make a chance tree for this situation. Use any number of cars you like.

   b. How much money would be collected in the situation you made for part **a**?

   c. What is the average toll charge per car on this toll road?

   d. If you start your chance tree in part **a** with a different number of cars, would your answer for part **c** change? Explain your thinking.

1 If different students begin with different numbers of cars, they can compare their results to check their thinking for part **d**.

Assessment Pyramid

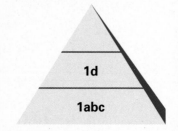

Assesses Section D Goals

Reaching All Learners

Parent Involvement

Have students share the Summary and their work at home. Students could ask their parents about any situations where they know that the expected value is used. Parents may have examples when the true results were quite different from the expected value.

Solutions and Samples

Answers to Check Your Work

1. a The chance tree you made for this situation may look like this.

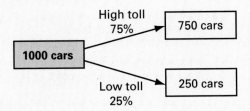

Since you could choose a number of cars to start with, you may have chosen another number. Your percentages should be the same because they do not depend on the number of cars but only on the fraction.

b. In the situation for part **a**, 750 × $3.00 + 250 × $1.00 = $2,500, so $2,500 in tolls is collected. If you used different numbers, your toll will be different as well.

c. The average amount that a car on this toll road pays is $\frac{\$2,500}{1000}$ = $2.50 per car. If you used a different number of cars, this amount will be the same.

d. No, the answer for part **c** will not change if the number of cars is different. For example, if there were 500 cars, the toll collected would be 375 × $3 + 125 × $1 = $1,250. This is $\frac{\$1,250}{500}$ = $2.50 per car. The average toll per car will always be the same because the toll per car depends on the percentage of cars for each option, which stays the same.

Hints and Comments

Overview

Students read the Summary, which reviews the main topics covered in this section. In Check your Work, students assess themselves on the concepts and skills from this section. Students can check their answers on Student Book pages 61 and 62.

Planning

After students finish Section D, you may assign as homework appropriate activities from the Additional Practice section, located on Student Book pages 53 and 54.

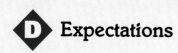

Expectations

Notes

3 This problem is similar to the mayfly problem. Have students think about a variety of ways to approach the problem in order to find the expected wait time.

2. Brenda is a basketball player. She is an 80% free-throw shooter.

   a. Make a chance tree to show how Brenda is expected to score in 100 two-point free-throw situations.

   b. What is the chance Brenda will score two points in a two-point free-throw situation?

3. The table contains data on how long customers have to wait in line for the bank teller. These data were collected from a sample of 100 customers.

Waiting Time (in minutes)	0	1	2	3	4	6	7	8	9	10
Number of Customers	24	16	9	7	6	8	8	11	9	2

   a. Based on the data, what is the chance a customer will have to wait in line?

   b. What is the chance that a customer must wait at least 6 minutes?

   c. Use the data to calculate the expected waiting time per customer.

   d. Is knowing the "expected waiting time per customer" useful? Why or why not?

 For Further Reflection

Write an explanation of expected value for someone in your family. Use examples to help the person understand what it is and how it might be used.

Assessment Pyramid

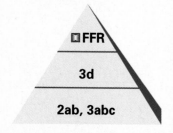

□FFR

3d

2ab, 3abc

Assesses Section D Goals

Reaching All Learners

Parent Involvement

Students should share their work on For Further Reflection with whoever they wrote it for. They could report back to the class on how well they were able to explain the concept.

Solutions and Samples

2. a See chance tree.

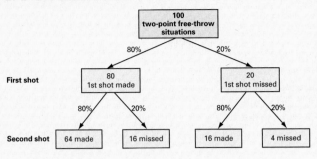

b. The chance Brenda will score two points in a two-point free-throw situation is 64 out of 100, which is 64%.

3. a. To compute the chance a customer will have to wait in line, the number of customers who have to wait in line longer than 0 minutes will be 100 − 24 or 76 customers, which is a 76% chance.

b. The chance that a customer must wait at least 6 minutes is $(8 + 8 + 11 + 9 + 2)/100$, which is 38%.

c. All 100 customers together waited $1 \times 16 + 2 \times 9 + 3 \times 7 + 4 \times 6 + 6 \times 8 + 7 \times 8 + 8 \times 11 + 9 \times 9 + 10 \times 2 = 372$ minutes. This is 3.72 minutes expected waiting time per customer.

d. Knowing the "expected waiting time per customer" can be useful if you want to have a one-number indication of how long people must wait. Bank managers are interested in serving their customers by trying to reduce waiting time but do not want tellers with nothing to do. It might be more useful in combination with measures of spread that would give an indication of how the wait time might vary for different customers. The shortest and longest waiting times might also be useful information.

For Further Reflection

Answers will vary. Sample answer:

Expected value is a kind of mean. If for example you know the chances of certain outcomes, like the chances on paying high toll and on paying low toll for cars, the expected amount of toll per car can be calculated.

First, the total expected toll for all cars can be calculated. From that, it is easy to calculate the expected toll that will be paid per car. Expected value is not an actual value that happens; no car will exactly

Hints and Comments

Overview

Students complete the Check Your Work problems from this section. Students can check their answers on Student Book pages 61 and 62. They reflect on the topics addressed in this section in the For Further Reflection problem.

Planning

After students finish Section D, you may assign as homework appropriate activities from the Additional Practice section, located on Student Book pages 53 and 54.

pay the expected value of toll. Each car either pays the high toll or low toll, and the expected value is taken over a larger number of cars. It can still be a useful value to compare or to predict.

Different toll situations can be compared by comparing the expected values for the tolls. You can use expected value in many situations, such as life expectancy, sports, and so on. The expected score a person will make is based on his or her "scoring average."

Section Focus

In this section students investigate situations in which two events occur and the chance of each event is known. They use diagrams, area models, and chance trees to investigate both dependent and independent events. Students calculate chances for combined events. The multiplication rule for chance is formalized. This section reviews topics addressed in the unit *Second Chance* and in previous sections of this unit.

Pacing and Planning

Day 16: Free Meal		Student pages 40–42
INTRODUCTION	Problem 1	Use fractions to estimate the probability of getting a free hot dog and free drink at a school event.
CLASSWORK	Problems 2–7	Conduct a simulation and use the results to estimate the probability of getting a free hot dog and free drink at a school event.
HOMEWORK	Problem 8	Use a chance tree to calculate the number of students getting a free hot dog and free drink at a school event.

Day 17: Free Meal (Continued)		Student pages 43–45
INTRODUCTION	Review homework.	Review homework from Day 16.
CLASSWORK	Problems 9–12	Use an area model to determine the probability of getting a free hot dog at a school event and to justify the multiplication rule for the probabilities of combined events.
HOMEWORK	Problem 13	Solve a problem where the fractions are not multiplied to determine the answer.

Day 18: Delayed Luggage		Student pages 45–49
INTRODUCTION	Review homework.	Review homework from Day 17.
CLASSWORK	Problems 14–18	Solve a probability and expected value problem involving the possibility of having delayed luggage on an airplane flight.
HOMEWORK	Check Your Work For Further Reflection	Find the chance for combined events using an area model.

Additional Resources: Additional Practice, Section E, Student Book page 54

Materials

Student Resources
No resources required

Teachers Resources
No resources required

Student Materials
Quantities listed are per student.

• Two different-colored number cubes

* See Hints and Comments for optional materials.

Learning Lines

Combined Events

Students continue the study of chances in combined event situations that they began in the unit *Second Chance*. They compare experimental chances for the combined event of getting a free drink and/or a free hot dog to the theoretical chance. They explore more complex situations using chance trees and area models. The multiplication rule for chances is formalized. Students find out that this rule will not always work, such as in the case of dependent events.

Models and Strategies

Students can structure multi-event situations by using a chance tree or an area model. These models were introduced and used in the unit *Second Chance*.

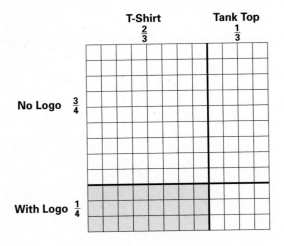

In the illustration at the bottom left, the area of the whole rectangle in the area model represents a chance of 1 as well as the total number of shirts that the problem is about (in this example 144). The area of each of the four parts into which the rectangle is divided represents the chance for the different combined outcomes. The chances of these outcomes can be found in two ways. For example, the chance of the combined event that a randomly chosen shirt is a T-shirt with a logo is 24 out of 144 (using the absolute numbers of small squares), which is $\frac{1}{6}$. Or it can be said to be $\frac{1}{4} \times \frac{2}{3}$ (using the chances, the fractional parts), which is also $\frac{1}{6}$.

Using the chance tree, a similar method can be used: calculating with the absolute numbers in the boxes or using the chances along the branches. For both models, when using the chances instead of the absolute numbers, the multiplication rule for chances is applied. Students discover that this rule can be used only if the events are (or can be made) independent.

At the End of This Section: Learning Outcomes

Students can calculate chances in multi-event situations using chance trees or an area model. The multiplication rule for chances (for independent events) is formalized in this unit.

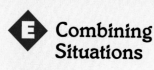

Combining Situations

Free Meal

The eighth graders at Takadona Middle School are organizing a Fun Night for all students in grades 7 and 8. There will be games, movies, and food for the students to enjoy. Each student who comes to Fun Night will receive one red coupon and one green coupon. Some of the red coupons will have a star, which can be turned in for a free hot dog. Similarly, some of the green coupons will have a star, which is good for a free drink. If a coupon does not have a star, it is good for a discount on a food or drink purchase.

The organizers want to give away enough coupons with stars on them so that the chance that a student will get a free hot dog is $\frac{1}{6}$, and the chance a student will get a free drink is $\frac{1}{2}$.

1. Choose a number of coupons you would make. How many would be red, green, with star, and without star to make these chances happen?

Before the coupons are made, the mathematics teacher asks the class to find the chance that a student will get *both* a free hot dog and a free drink.

2. What do you think the chance of getting both will be?

2 This problem is intended to be students' first impressions. However, you may want to briefly discuss the different ways that the chance could be expressed: percents, fractions, decimals, and proportions.

Reaching All Learners

Intervention

If students think the probability is $\frac{1}{4}$ because there are four outcomes, you might want to begin to draw a tree to show the possibilities. You could also refer back to the two-point free-throw problem where the chance of making each shot made quite a difference on the expected value.

Solutions and Samples

1. Answers will vary depending on what number of visitors the students expect. Sample answer:

   I choose to make 300 coupons. Since each student will get one red and one green coupon, they could make 150 red and 150 green. $\frac{1}{6}$ of the 150 red ones, 25 coupons, will have a star. $\frac{1}{2}$ of the 150 green ones, 75 coupons will have a star.

2. Answers may vary, but the correct answer is about 8%. Sample strategy multiplying the chances: $\frac{1}{2} \times \frac{1}{6} = \frac{1}{12}$, or 8%.

Hints and Comments

Overview

Students are introduced to the context of a Fun Night at a middle school. Students guess the chance that a student at Fun Night will receive coupons for both a free hot dog and a free drink.

About the Mathematics

Students were introduced to probability represented as a fraction in the unit *Take a Chance*, and they worked with chances as fractions in the unit *Second Chance*. They usually used fractions in chance trees in that unit. Students revisit the situation of combined events, either events in a sequence or simultaneous events. They were introduced to the use of chance trees and an area model to calculate chances on combined events in the unit *Second Chance*. This is revisited and expanded in this section.

Planning

Students may work on problem 1 individually; you may want to discuss students' choices in a whole-class discussion. Problem 2 can be done n the same way.

Comments About the Solutions

1. In this problem, students reason from a chance to an actual number of favorable and possible outcomes to find this chance. Be sure the fractional parts are calculated correctly. You may want to discuss what numbers are easy and why.

2. Students have calculated chances for combined events in the unit *Second Chance*. They used chance trees and the area model to help them structure the situation and calculate the chances. They also used the rule for multiplication of chances. Students may find the correct answer by using the numbers of coupons they suggested for problem 1 and calculating the chance as the ratio of favorable outcomes to the total number of outcomes.

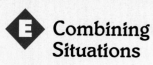 Combining Situations

Notes

3 Be sure students agree within each group on what different results on the number cubes will mean in terms of the free food.

4 It is critical that students have a chart that will be efficient to use before they start the activity. Students may be tempted to record only "yes, both free" and "no, they were not." These answers will not give students the data they will need to answer some of the later questions.

6 Students may have to convert their answers to the same form, decimals, percents, fractions, or ratios, to make comparisons.

It is possible to do a simulation to estimate the chance that a student gets both a free hot dog and a free drink. Instead of actually making coupons and handing them out, the class decides to use two different colored number cubes: a red one and a green one.

Each roll of the number cubes generates a pair of numbers. The outcome of the red number cube is for the red coupons; the outcome of the green one is for the green coupons.

3. Describe how the outcomes of the number cubes can represent the stars for a free meal and a free drink.

You are going to generate 100 pairs of numbers with the two number cubes to simulate 100 students arriving at Fun Night.

4. Design a chart that will make it easy to record the results. The chart should show clearly what each student gets: a free hot dog, a free drink, both, or none.

Activity

Use the two different colored number cubes and the chart you designed in problem 4.

Try a few rolls with the number cubes to make sure that your chart works.

Generate 100 pairs of numbers with the number cubes and record the results in your chart. Every possible pair of outcomes on the number cubes should fall into one of the possibilities on your chart.

5. Use your simulation results to estimate:

   a. the chance that a student gets a free hot dog;

   b. the chance that a student gets a free drink; and

   c. the chance that a student gets a free hot dog and a free drink.

6. How close was your answer to problem 2 to the results of the simulation?

Assessment Pyramid

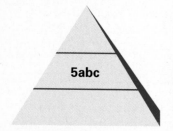

5abc

Use simulation and modeling to investigate probability.

Reaching All Learners

Accommodation

It may be necessary to provide a ready-made chart for problem 4 for some students. It may also make sense to have some students only do 50 or even 25 pairs and then combine the information.

Solutions and Samples

3. Answers will vary. A sample answer:
For the green number cube, the chance of a star/free drink must be $\frac{1}{2}$, so three numbers on the green number cube must represent this chance. For instance the numbers 1, 2, and 3 can represent the chance of a free drink. For the red coupons, the chance of a star (free hot dog) must be $\frac{1}{6}$, so one of the numbers on the red number cube, for instance the 1, can represent a star.

4. Charts will vary. Sample chart, with a sample set of simulation results:

First Cube (Red)	Second Cube (Green)	Meaning	Frequency	Total
1	1, 2, or 3	free hot dog and free drink	⌿⌿⌿ ⌿⌿⌿ I	11
1	4, 5, or 6	free hot dog only	⌿⌿⌿ III	8
2, 3, 4, 5, or 6	1, 2, or 3	free drink only	⌿⌿⌿ ⌿⌿⌿ ⌿⌿⌿ ⌿⌿⌿ ⌿⌿⌿ ⌿⌿⌿ ⌿⌿⌿ IIII	39
2, 3, 4, 5, or 6	4, 5, or 6	nothing free	⌿⌿⌿ ⌿⌿⌿ ⌿⌿⌿ ⌿⌿⌿ ⌿⌿⌿ ⌿⌿⌿ ⌿⌿⌿ II	42

5. Answers will vary. Sample responses using the chart from problem 4:

a. The frequency of getting a free hot dog (number of favorable outcomes) is the sum of the first two rows: 19.

So the chance of getting a free hot dog based on these results is $\frac{19}{100}$.

b. The frequency of getting a free drink (number of favorable outcomes) is the total of the first and third rows, $39 + 11$, or 50. The chance of getting a free drink based on these results is $\frac{50}{100}$, or $\frac{1}{2}$.

c. The frequency of getting both a free hot dog and a free drink is found in row 1; it is 11. The chance of getting both a free hot dog and a free drink is $\frac{11}{100}$.

6. Answers will vary, depending on the answer to problem 5. Sample answer:

The chance calculated for problem 2 was 1 out of 12 or 8%. The chance found in the simulation was 11 out of 100 or 11%. These chances are close but different.

Hints and Comments

Materials

Two different-colored number cubes one pair per student;
graphing calculators or other random-number generator, optional (one per group of students)

Overview

Students design an experiment using number cubes to simulate the situation of giving away free drinks and free hot dogs. They investigate the chances of the different outcomes.

About the Mathematics

The advantage of a simulation is that data can be obtained without doing the real experiment. Rolling number cubes helps to make the simulation occur as it would in real life (assuming that in real life things also happen randomly). Designing and organizing the simulation and using diagrams and charts to collect and represent the data are essential if you want to make predictions about the situation. They have used simulations in the units *Insights into Data* and *Second Chance*. The chances based on data from an experiment are called experimental or empirical chances; calculated chances are called theoretical chances. If a simulation is done a large number of times, the experimental probabilities (relative frequencies of the outcomes) will approach the theoretical chances.

Planning

Students may work on problems 3 and 4 in pairs or small groups. Discuss students' answers to these problems in class to make sure all students use a correct simulation and have a chart that can be used to record the results. Students can then work in pairs on the Activity and problems 5 and 6.

Comments About the Solutions

Activity

The colors of the number cubes are not important, but two different colors are needed to distinguish the outcomes. Instead of using number cubes, pairs of random numbers from 1–6 can be generated using a graphing calculator. You can have each student generate 100 outcomes; you may also split the 100 outcomes over two or four students in a group. Encourage students to code their results and record the code rather than trying to remember what number they used to represent what outcome.

5. Students can find the chance of each outcome as the relative frequencies of that outcome; they did this in the unit *Second Chance*.

E Combining Situations

Notes

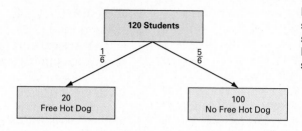

120 Students

$\frac{1}{6}$ $\frac{5}{6}$

20 Free Hot Dog   **100 No Free Hot Dog**

Dianne complains that the simulation takes too long. She suggests using a chance tree like the one shown to represent the problem.

Suppose 120 students attend Fun Night. Then 20 students will get free hot dogs, and 100 will not get free hot dogs.

7. Explain how you would find the numbers 20 and 100.

Each student who gets a free hot dog has a chance of $\frac{1}{2}$ to get a free drink as well.

7 The simulation activity produced results that can be used to estimate the probabilities. In this problem, the actual expected values are calculated to give the theoretical probability results. If the simulation is done enough times, the two results should be very close. However, by chance, simulation may give a very different outcome.

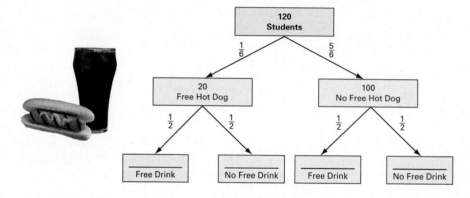

120 Students

$\frac{1}{6}$ $\frac{5}{6}$

20 Free Hot Dog   **100 No Free Hot Dog**

$\frac{1}{2}$ $\frac{1}{2}$ $\frac{1}{2}$ $\frac{1}{2}$

Free Drink   **No Free Drink**   **Free Drink**   **No Free Drink**

8a Students have used this type of chance tree with percents in Section D of this unit. They used fractions in chance trees in the unit *Second Chance*.

8. a. Copy and complete the chance tree.

b. How many students receive a "free meal" consisting of both a free hot dog and a free drink?

c. From your chance tree, what is the chance of receiving a free meal?

d. Reflect How does the chance that you found in part **c** compare to the chance you found in problem 2 and the one that you found using the simulation in problem 5?

e. Reflect If you started the chance tree about Fun Night with 300 students instead of 120, would your answers for **c** change? Why or why not?

Assessment Pyramid

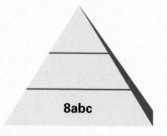

8abc

Use chance trees to find probability.

Reaching All Learners

Act It Out

You could act out the theoretical situation with a group of 12 or 24 students.

Intervention

For problem 8e, you might want to point out to students the advantage of using a common multiple as a starting number. The end results will produce equivalent ratios, no matter what number was used at the start.

Solutions and Samples

7. 20 is $\frac{1}{6}$ of 120, and 100 is 120−20, which can also be found as $\frac{5}{6}$ of 120.

8. a.

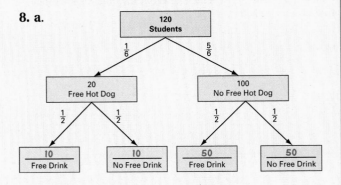

b. According to the diagram, 10 students will receive a free hot dog and a free drink.

c. The chance of receiving a free meal is $\frac{10}{120}$, or $\frac{1}{12}$.

d. Answers will vary. Sample answer:

In problem 5, the simulated response was an $\frac{11}{100}$ or 11% (experimental) chance on a free meal; using the diagram, the theoretical chance was $\frac{1}{12}$ or 8%. This was the same as in problem 2.

e. No, this will make no difference in the chance. Now 50 students will receive a free hot dog, and of these, half or 25 students will also receive a free drink. So the chance is $\frac{25}{300} = \frac{1}{12}$, which is 8%. This is the same. Because the fractions have the same value, the chance will also be the same.

Hints and Comments

Overview

Students use chance trees to calculate the theoretical chance for getting a free hot dog or a free drink.

About the Mathematics

On the previous page, Student Book page 41, students designed a simulation to get data that could be used to estimate chances. This is called experimental or empirical probability. Another way to find the chances is through reasoning (using theoretical probability), without doing a simulation or experiment. Students do so on this page, where they use a chance tree to calculate the chances for combined events, two outcomes both occurring. The chances found both ways are compared, and students reason about the differences they found.

Planning

Students may work on problems 7 and 8 individually or in pairs.

Comments About the Solutions

7. The numbers 20 and 100 are the expected numbers of students to receive a free hot dog or not, based on the theoretical chances.

8. d. On the previous page students used a simulation to estimate the chances on a free drink, a free hot dog, both, or neither. In part **c,** the theoretical chance on the combined outcome is calculated. If the simulation is done enough times, the two results should be very close. However, by chance, due to variation in the outcomes, simulations may give very different chances.

e. Be sure students understand the significance of using a common multiple as a starting number. The end results will produce equivalent ratios no matter what number was used at the start. The chances are the relative frequencies, they only depend on the fractions (chances) used with the branches in the tree. Some students may remember that they can also find the chances without using a starting number.

E Combining Situations

Notes

You may also advise some students to make a chance tree and see if they can find a number that will work there. If students chose 120 because this was used before, ask them if they know a smaller number that will also work.

9 Students may have seen an area model before and may realize that the process here is multiplication.

Kiesha wanted to use another model to find the chance. She thought an area model might work. This is the series of drawings Kiesha made for the situation on Fun Night.

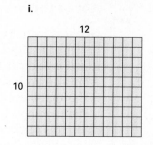

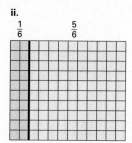

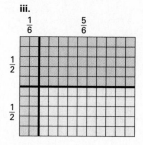

9. a. How many students does each diagram represent? Why do you think this number is chosen?

   b. What do grids ii and iii show in terms of the tickets for Fun Night?

   c. Copy grid iii into your notebook and shade the portion of the diagram that represents the students who get a free meal.

   d. How do the diagrams help you find the fractional part of the students who get a free meal?

   e. How does this help you find the chance of a free meal (hotdog and drink)?

The organizers of Fun Night are worried about cost. They have decided to change the number of tickets with stars so that the chance of getting a free hot dog will be $\frac{1}{8}$ and the chance of a free drink will be $\frac{1}{3}$.

10. a. Draw an area model to represent this situation. Think about a good number of small squares to use!

   b. Use your area model to find the chance of getting both a free hot dog and free drink in this new situation.

10 This problem provides a chance for students to try the technique again. Be sure that they approach part **a** carefully since choosing a number that is not a common multiple of 8 and 3 will make the problem much more difficult.

Assessment Pyramid

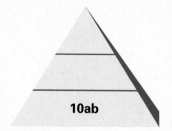

Use area models to find probability.

Reaching All Learners

Accommodation

Providing a copy of chart **iii** may be helpful for some students rather than having them copy the whole thing. For others, providing graph paper may be sufficient.

Solutions and Samples

9. a. The diagram represents the 120 students. Each cell is one student. Reasons may vary. Sample reasons:

- This is the same number used in the chance tree on the previous page.
- It is a number that can be divided in sixths and in halves.

b. The second grid shows that $\frac{1}{6}$ of the students (left of the vertical line) get a free hot dog, and $\frac{5}{6}$ (right of the line) get no free hot dog. The third grid shows that half of the students (the part above—or under—the horizontal line) get a free drink, and the other half get no free drink

c. The double shaded part in the lower left corner, represents the students who get a free meal: free drink and free hot dog.

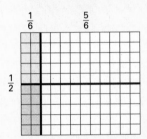
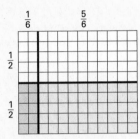

d. You can determine what part of the grid is shaded both times. This part represents students who get a free meal. This is 10 out of the 120 squares, so it is $\frac{10}{120}$, or $\frac{1}{12}$.

e. The chance of getting a free meal is the same as the fractional part found in **d**, the relative frequency, so the chance of a free meal is $\frac{10}{120}$, or $\frac{1}{12}$.

10. a. Sample area model with 24 squares:

b. The chance of getting both a free hot dog and a free drink is $\frac{1}{24}$.

Hints and Comments

Overview

Students use area models to model the situation of the free drink and free hot dog at Fun Night. They use the model to calculate chances on combined outcomes.

About the Mathematics

The area model was introduced in the unit *Second Chance* as a model to find chances for situations with combined events. The area model has the same number of units as a starting number in the chance tree. This area model may also be seen as a concrete version of the two-way tables and charts used in Section B. Area models were also used in some Number units to help students visualize the multiplication of fractions.

Planning

Students may work on problems 9 and 10 individually or in pairs.

Comments About the Solutions

9. Students must understand how the area model is divided in two directions to represent the relative frequencies (chances) of the combinations of the outcomes for the two events. You may refer students to other units in which the area model was used.

E Combining Situations

Notes

11 This problem gives students a chance to combine what they have learned and apply the strategies to a new situation. Observe the strategies students use to gauge their understanding of the concepts.

12 Students should be able to relate the area model to multiplication and thus understand why multiplying the chances makes sense. Many students will have observed this prior to the statement; this problem gives them a chance to justify it.

One of the events for Fun Night is a student volleyball tournament. The Fun Night Committee plans to give the players on the winning team shirts donated by the Takadona Sports Apparel Mart.

There will be both tank tops and T-shirts.

Two-thirds ($\frac{2}{3}$) of all the shirts will be T-shirts.

Logos will be applied randomly to $\frac{1}{4}$ of all shirts.

After the tournament, the winning captain can pull one shirt out of the box.

11. What is the chance that the shirt will be a T-shirt with a logo? Show the method you used to find your answer.

One way to find the chance of an event is to list all the possible results and count them, but this is often very time-consuming. Here is a rule that seems to work: The chance for a combination of two events to occur is the chance of the first event times the chance of the second event. We can call this a **multiplication rule for chance**.

12. a. Does the rule work for problems 10 and 11?

b. Reflect How does this rule show up in the chance tree and the area model?

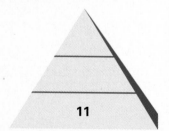
Reaching All Learners

Intervention

Students who are struggling with problem 11 should make a chance tree or an area model first.

Solutions and Samples

11. The chance that the shirt is a T-shirt with a logo is $\frac{1}{6}$. Strategies will vary. Sample strategy using an area model:

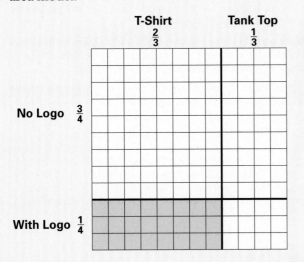

The chance of a T-shirt with a logo can be found as the double shaded part in the lower left.

The chance is the ratio of the 24 squares that satisfy both conditions (favorable outcomes) to all 144 squares in the grid (all possible outcomes). This is 24 out of 144 or $\frac{24}{144} = \frac{2}{12} = \frac{1}{6}$.

12. a. Yes, for problem 10, $\frac{1}{8} \times \frac{1}{3} = \frac{1}{24}$. For problem 11, $\frac{2}{3} \times \frac{1}{4} = \frac{2}{12} = \frac{1}{6}$.

  b. In the chance tree, you multiply the chances along the branches. You can see this in the splitting of the numbers in the boxes. In the area model, you may find the area of the shaded part by multiplying length times width using fractions, which will give you a fraction (as part of the whole rectangle) for the double shaded part. This is the chance of the combination of outcomes.

Hints and Comments

Overview

Students investigate another situation about chances of combined events. The rule for multiplying chances is formalized.

About the Mathematics

The multiplication rule for chances that was pre-formally introduced in the unit *Second Chance* is formalized here. The chance of two events occurring is the chance of the first event times the chance of the second event. Students connect the use of this rule to the area model and the chance tree. They need to understand how to multiply fractions. This is addressed in the Number strand.

Planning

Students may work on problems 11 and 12 individually or in pairs. After students finish these problems you may want to discuss problem 12b and the multiplication rule with the class.

Comments About the Solutions

12. You may have students look back to other problems as well. Some students may never have used the multiplication rule before. Ask them to check whether they would get the same answer if they did. If students have difficulty multiplying fractions, you may want to have a class discussion on how to do this. This topic is addressed in several of the units in the Number strand, and in the *Number Tools* resource as well.

Combining Situations

Notes

13 The purpose of this problem is to show that the multiplication rule, discussed on the previous page, does not work if the events are connected in any way. In formal probability language, if the events are independent, you can multiply the probabilities. Students should be able to connect this to their work in the previous sections.

14 You may want to ask students to write the probability using several different representations.

Suppose the Takadona Sports Apparel Mart has discovered that the logos do not fit very well on the tank tops. They realize that they can only put logos on T-shirts. Two thirds of the shirts will still be T-shirts, and $\frac{1}{4}$ of all of the shirts will still have logos

13. a. Choose a total number of shirts. Make a diagram to show how many of these are tank tops, how many are T-shirts, and how many are T-shirts with logos.

  b. If you select one of these shirts at random, what is the chance that it will be a T-shirt with a logo?

  c. Does this problem follow the multiplication rule? What makes this situation different from the situation in problem 11?

Overall, if there is no connection between getting one outcome and getting the other, then you can use the multiplication rule to find the chance that both events will happen. Otherwise, you have to use some other method to find the chance, like you did in problem 13.

Delayed Luggage

Vernon is planning a trip over winter break. He is excited about traveling by plane, but he has heard stories about people's luggage being delayed. He is wondering what the chances are that he will fly to his vacation spot without having his luggage delayed. Through a little research, he found that about 1 out of every 200 pieces of luggage is delayed per flight.

14. What is the chance that a piece of luggage will arrive on time on a one-way trip?

Reaching All Learners

Parent Involvement

You could have students ask their relatives or friends whether they have ever lost luggage on a trip. Students can use the data they gather to check the information that one out of every 200 pieces of luggage gets lost. Students can also find information on current rates from the U.S. Department of Transportation.

Solutions and Samples

13. a. Answers will vary. Sample answer:

If there are 12 shirts, 8 will be T-shirts since 8 is two thirds of 12. Because $\frac{1}{4}$ of all the shirts have logos and the logos can only be on T-shirts, $\frac{1}{4}$ of the 12 shirts, which is three of the eight T-shirts, will have logos.

This is shown in the chance tree diagram.

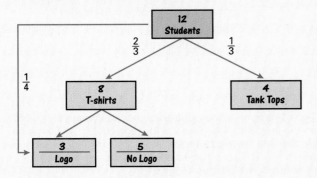

b. The chance that the shirt chosen will be a T-shirt with a logo is 3 out of 12, or $\frac{1}{4}$.

c. Answers will vary. Sample response:

You cannot multiply $\frac{2}{3} \times \frac{1}{4}$ to find the correct chance. This can be seen for example in the chance tree. The $\frac{1}{4}$ is at the same "level" in the tree as $\frac{2}{3}$; you don't pass the two fractions when you follow the route in the tree.

The situation is different than the one in problem 11 since there is a connection between having a logo and a T-shirt. Logos go on T-shirts, so these events are dependent. In the other case, getting a free drink did not have any connection to getting a free hot dog.

14. The chance is 199 in 200, or 99.5%.

Hints and Comments

Overview

Students determine how many shirts are T-shirts and how many T-shirts have logos. They determine the chance that a T-shirt selected at random will have a logo. Then, they explain why this problem does not follow the multiplication rule. Next they investigate chances of losing luggage on a flight.

About the Mathematics

Chance trees, area models, and systematic lists of the possibilities often help students to visualize the problem situation. When all possibilities are listed, it is not difficult to find the appropriate chances. Because listing the possibilities can be very time-consuming however, it is often faster to use a rule or formula, like the rule for multiplication of chances. However, this rule will not work for dependent events. So it is not very wise to just multiply chances in situations with combined events. Making a drawing of the situation before using such a rule will help clarify the situation and decide whether events may be dependent and how chances must be found.

Planning

Students may work on problem 13 individually. Discuss the answers in class. You may read the text about lost luggage in class; students can work on problem 14 individually.

E Combining Situations

Notes

17 As they think about these problems, students may have ideas about situations in which the probabilities are added. They may also realize that it is possible to work backwards—using the complement of an event to find the probability.

18 The problem can be solved using the multiplication rule, but not in the same way as on the previous pages. Since the same piece of luggage cannot get lost on both the first and the second flight, it is not possible to calculate a meaningful chance by multiplying 1/200 by 1/200.

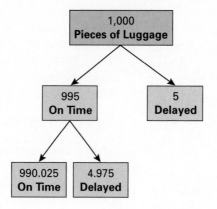

Vernon wants to find the chance that his luggage will make it without any delay on a trip that has one layover. (During a layover, people and luggage often change planes.) He decides to use a tree diagram. He begins by thinking about 1,000 pieces of luggage.

Vernon concludes that, in all, about 990 pieces of luggage will make it without any delay on a trip that has one layover.

15. Explain the numbers in the diagram. Add chances to the branches.

Richard, one of Vernon's friends, questions his calculations. He points out that on the first flight, five pieces of luggage out of a 1,000 will be delayed. And on the second flight, five pieces out of 1,000 should also be delayed. This means that exactly ten pieces are delayed, so 990 pieces of luggage will arrive on time.

While Vernon's and Richard's answers are close, their calculations are different.

16. Which method of calculation, Vernon's or Richard's, do you think is correct?

17. a. To explore the two different methods, use both Vernon's and Richard's methods to calculate the number of pieces of luggage that are not delayed on a trip with one layover if 1 out of every 5 pieces is delayed on every flight. Start your diagram with 1,000 pieces of luggage.

b. Based on your results, which method do you think is correct?

18. Can you use the multiplication rule to solve Vernon's problem? Why or why not?

Assessment Pyramid

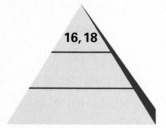

16, 18

Develop and use a critical attitude toward the use of probability.

Reaching All Learners

Intervention

When working with problem 16, students may give a wrong answer, based just on what they think. You may ask them to make up numbers for the chances for which both methods will give a different result. You can also leave the wrong answers. In problem 17, they will investigate the situation by using a chance tree.

Solutions and Samples

15. Explanations will vary. Sample explanation: 995 pieces out of 1,000 of the luggage (which is the same as 199 out of every 200, or 99.5%) will arrive on time, and five pieces out of 1,000 (or 1 out of every 200, or 0.5%) will be delayed. I used the same ratios for the second flight. When 0.5% is taken from 995 pieces of luggage, 990 pieces are left and 5 are delayed. These numbers should be rounded because a fraction of a piece of luggage cannot be delayed. The first two branches have 99.5% and 0.5% chances. The second set has the same.

16. Vernon's method of calculation is correct. Richard's method does not take the five pieces that have already been delayed into account. Both methods result in the same answer in this instance, because of the small percentage for delayed luggage and the rounding that needs to be done, but Richard's method will not always work.

17 a. Vernon's method:

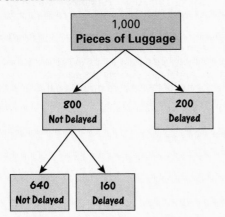

There were 640 pieces of luggage that were not delayed.

Richard's method: 200 pieces of luggage were delayed on the first flight, and 200 were delayed on the second flight. There were 400 pieces of luggage delayed, so there were 600 that were not delayed.

b. Vernon's method: Students should understand the error in Richard's method. Richard's method assumes that an equal number are delayed on the second flight, even though there are fewer bags.

18. You can use the multiplication rule since the events are independent. The chance that a piece of luggage will make both trips without any delay is $\frac{199}{200} \times \frac{199}{200} \quad \frac{39,601}{40,000} \approx 99\%$.

Hints and Comments

Overview

Students continue investigating the chances of losing luggage using several methods.

About the Mathematics

In probability it is very easy to reason in the wrong way. A common mistake is to take the wrong set of all possible outcomes or, for a sequence of events, to neglect to take into account what happened in the first event. If, for example, an event occurs twice, the chance is the second time may be influenced by what happened the first time. This of course is not always the case; it is wise to check if the events are dependent. On this page, in the context of delayed luggage, students compare two ways of reasoning about chances and decide which is the correct way.

Planning

Students may work on problems 15–18 individually or in pairs.

Did You Know?

The Bureau of Transportation Statistics (website: http://www.bts.gov/) collects data each month on several aspects of travel. One of their subjects is mishandled luggage. Almost every month, an Air Travel Consumer Report is published by The Office of Aviation Enforcement and Proceedings, Aviation Consumer Protection Division, that has a chapter with statistics of mishandled luggage. These reports can be found on the Internet. http://airconsumer.ost.dot.gov/reports/index.htm.

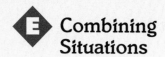

Math History

Christiaan Huygens

Christiaan Huygens (1629–1695) was a Dutch scientist who made a major contribution to several fields of science. He studied law and mathematics at the University of Leiden. After writing several math books, Huygens worked on lens grinding and telescope construction. He found a better way of grinding and polishing lenses. Using one of his own lenses, Huygens detected the first moon of Saturn. Since his work in astronomy required accurate time-keeping, Huygens worked on making a clock. In 1656 he patented the first pendulum clock. This clock greatly increased the accuracy of time measurement.

In 1655 Huygens visited Paris and learned about the work on probability carried out in correspondence between two other mathematicians, Pascal (1623–1662) and Fermat (1601–1665).

On his return to Holland in 1656, Huygens wrote a book on the calculations of chances. It was a small book of about 15 pages and the first printed work on the subject in 1655. It was translated into English in 1692.

The book, *Of The Laws of Chance or A Method of Calculation of the Hazards of Game...,* contains theory on probability calculations and 14 problems with solutions and five problems to be solved by the reader. Some of the chance problems that you have seen in this unit are in this book.

Reaching All Learners

Study Skills

Before reading the Summary, ask students to identify three ideas from this unit that were new to them. This helps students think about what they have learned and also gives you some valuable insights.

Hints and Comments

Overview

Students read the Math History. There are no problems on this page for students to solve.

Combining Situations

Notes

At this point, students should be clear about the connections between the different models and when each is appropriate. Spend some time discussing each of the models and which are useful when.

Summary >>―――

In this section, you explored two-event probability problems. Sometimes you can calculate the chance of a combined event from the chances of the underlying events.

To find the chances for two combined events you can use several methods:

- **a chance tree**

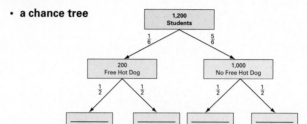

- **an area model**

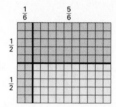

- **the multiplication rule**

    For example: The chance of getting a T-shirt is $\frac{2}{3}$, and the chance of getting a logo is $\frac{1}{4}$, so the chance of a T-shirt with a logo is $\frac{1}{4} \times \frac{2}{3}$, which is $\frac{2}{12}$ or $\frac{1}{6}$.

Note that not all three methods can be used in all situations.

If the two events are independent and do not affect each other, such as putting logos on all of the shirts and being a T-shirt or a tank top, then the chances of each event can be multiplied to find the chance that both events will occur.

If the two events are dependent, such as putting logos only on T-shirts, then you cannot multiply the two chances but must find another way to figure the chance that both events will occur.

Reaching All Learners

Parent Involvement

Have students explain the models to their parents.

Hints and Comments

Overview

Students read the Summary, which reviews the main topics covered in this section. There are no problems on this page for students to solve.

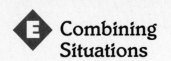

Check Your Work

The diagram illustrates all possible coupon combinations at Fun Night.

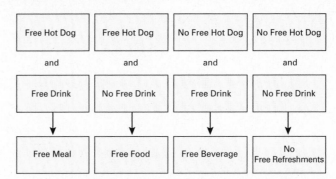

| Free Hot Dog | Free Hot Dog | No Free Hot Dog | No Free Hot Dog |

and · and · and · and

| Free Drink | No Free Drink | Free Drink | No Free Drink |

↓ · ↓ · ↓ · ↓

| Free Meal | Free Food | Free Beverage | No Free Refreshments |

1. **a.** Using the original probabilities of $\frac{1}{6}$ for a free hot dog and $\frac{1}{2}$ for a free drink, find the chance of getting something free.

   b. There are many ways to solve part **a.** Think of as many different ways as possible to solve this problem.

2. Make up a problem in which you can multiply the chances of two events happening and another problem in which you cannot. Explain the difference between the two problems.

3. Will and Robin are practicing free throws. Will has a 50% free-throw average, and Robin has a 70% average. They each take one shot.

   Use an area model to find the chance that both Will and Robin will make their shots.

For Further Reflection

Describe the advantages and disadvantages of using an area model to find the chance of two events. Of using a chance tree.

Reaching All Learners

Intervention

If students are having difficulty coming up with contexts for problem 2, have them look back though the unit to get ideas.

Solutions and Samples

Answers to Check Your Work

1. a and **b.**

The chance of getting something free is $\frac{7}{12}$. You might answer this problem in lots of ways. You may set up a diagram like the following.

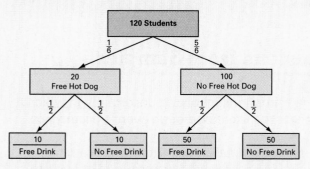

The number of students who will get something free is 20 + 50 = 70, so the chance of getting something free is $\frac{70}{120}$.

A clever way to find the answer is to think that the chance of getting something free is the complement of getting nothing free; out of 120 people, 50 will get nothing free, so there will be 120 − 50, or 70 out of 120 people, who will get something free. You might think of other ways as well.

2. You can make up many different problems. Be sure that the two events in the problem using the multiplication rule are independent, that is, not connected. Share your problems with a classmate.

Here is one example.

You could find the chance of getting heads twice when you toss two coins by multiplying the chance of getting heads on the first toss ($\frac{1}{2}$) times the chance of getting heads on the second toss ($\frac{1}{2}$) for a chance of $\frac{1}{4}$. The outcome of the first coin toss is not connected to the outcome of the second.

The two events in the problem where you cannot use the multiplication rule must be connected or overlap. For example, a class of 30 students is half girls, and one third of the class has blonde hair. So 15 of the students are girls, and 10 in the class have blonde hair. If you multiplied the chances of choosing a blonde-haired girl, it would be $\frac{1}{2} \times \frac{1}{3}$, or $\frac{1}{6}$ or 5 out of 30. But you cannot tell how many of the blondes are girls—all ten of the blondes could be girls. You need some more information to find the chance of choosing a blonde girl.

Hints and Comments

Overview

In Check Your Work, students assess themselves on the concepts and skills from this section. Students can check their answers on Student Book page 63. They reflect on the topics addressed in this section in the For Further Reflection problem.

Planning

After students finish Section E, you may assign as homework appropriate activities for homework from the Additional Practice section, located on Student Book page 5.

3. In the vertical direction, 70% (70 out of 100) is shaded to show Robin's chance of scoring. Of that part, the upper half is shaded to show Will's 50% chance of scoring. This means that the chance both will score is 35 out of 100, or 35%.

For Further Reflection

Answers will vary. Sample answer:

An advantage of the area model is that you can make the model in such a way that you can use the absolute number of small squares. You then do not have to multiply fractions or percents, but you can use the ratio of the number of small squares shaded for certain combinations of outcomes to the total number of small squares.

A disadvantage of using the area model is that you can only make it for situations with two events combined; if there are more, the area model cannot be used in the same way.

An advantage of a chance tree is that you can use it for more than two events. A disadvantage is that sometimes it is hard to draw and that you may have to multiply fractions to find chances on combined outcomes.

Additional Practice

Section Ⓐ Drawing Conclusions from Samples

1. Describe at least three situations involving uncertainty in which it is important to estimate the likelihood of an event's occurrence.

2. Think back to the questions on television ratings in this section. Do you think that the ratings computed are accurate enough to be used to decide how much to charge for an advertisement? Explain why or why not.

Suppose that a particular television station wants to know whether to add another half-hour of news to its evening broadcast. During the evening news for several nights, the announcers ask people to call a toll-free number to say whether or not they want an extra half-hour of news. The result of the poll was that a large majority voted in favor of extending the evening news.

3. **a.** If you were in favor of the expansion, what argument would you make?

   b. If you were against the expansion, what argument would you make?

In the small town of Arens (population 2,000), a journalist from the local newspaper went to the park and surveyed 100 people about building a recreation center on one side of town. Twenty-five people said they would like the center. The next day the journalist wrote an article about this issue with the headline:

> **A Large Majority of the People in Arens Do NOT Want a Recreation Center."**

4. **a.** Is this headline a fair statement? Explain your answer.

   A television reporter wanted to conduct her own survey. She called a sample of 20 people, whose names she randomly selected from the Arens telephone directory. Sixty percent said they were in favor of the recreation center.

   b. Is it reasonable to say that 60% of all the people in Arens are in favor of the recreation center? Explain why or why not.

   c. Describe how you would try to find out how many of the people in Arens want a recreation center. Explain why you think your method works.

Section A. Drawing Conclusions from Samples

1. Answers will vary. Sample responses:

- In football, it is important to have some sense of what the offense will do (pass or run) so you can set up your defense.

- In planning a trip, it is important to know whether it is likely to rain so you know whether or not to bring an umbrella.

- People who live along a river need to know whether the river is likely to flood during the spring so they can make preparations in case it does.

2. Answers will vary. Sample responses:

- No, because there were not enough people in the survey.

- No, because people can manipulate the results of the survey.

- Yes, because this is how Nielsen Media Research collected information, so it must work to some degree.

- Yes, because it uses random samples.

  You may suggest that you would need more information to decide how much to charge for an advertisement.

3. a. Different answers are possible. For example, you could say that the majority of the people who responded favored the expansion.

b. Answers will vary. Sample response:

The number of people watching may not have been sufficient to make a decision based on their views. If only 20 people were watching, a large majority of them would still not be a large number of people. Also, the sample was not chosen randomly. Only those watching had the opportunity to call in, and of those, only those who chose to call in were part of the survey. The survey excluded those who did not watch the evening broadcast.

4. a. Answers and explanations will vary. Sample response:

The people were not chosen randomly. The people who were not at the park that day had no chance to respond to the survey. Also, the people surveyed might live near the proposed recreation center and think it would be good to build it . The headline is based on the sample, so it may not be a fair statement.

b. Answers and explanations will vary. Sample response:

It may not be reasonable to say that 60% of the people in Arens are in favor of a recreation center. The method of choosing the sample seems to be fair. But the sample is very small, so the percent of the population in favor of a recreation center may still be different from the 60% quoted in the survey.

c. Answers and explanations will vary. Students should suggest that a sample be random, where everyone has a chance to respond, and not too small. If students suggest asking all the people in Arens, you might ask them to compare this method to taking a sample, considering the following factors: the survey method (how they want to reach everyone), the number of people who will not respond, the time it will take, and the reliability.

Section **B** May be There is a Connection

Benjamin has a drawer in which he keeps his pens and pencils. They come in different colors. He counts the pens and pencils and finds that there are 40 pencils, 12 of which are black, 8 are red, and the rest are blue. There are 20 pens. Eight pens are black, 2 are red, and the rest are blue.

1. Organize the information in a table.

2. a. If Benjamin takes one item out of his drawer at random, what is the chance that it is a pencil?

b. If Benjamin takes one item out of his drawer at random, what is the chance that it is red? Show how you found your answer.

c. If Benjamin chose a pencil in part **b**, is your answer the same?

Section **C** Reasoning from Samples

Here is a histogram of the speed of 63 cars at a road close to the Bora Middle School.

1. a. Estimate the chance that a car randomly chosen from this sample is driving faster than 30 mi/h.

b. Based on your answer to **a**, how can you easily calculate the chance that a car is driving 30 mi/h or slower?

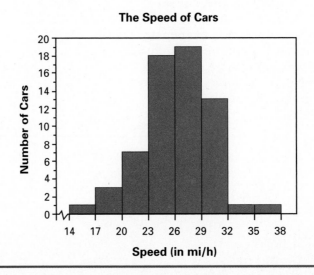

The Speed of Cars

Section B. May be There is a Connection

1. Sample table:

	Black	Red	Blue	Total
Pens	8	2	10	20
Pencils	12	8	20	40
Total	20	10	30	60

2. **a.** The chance that Benjamin will take a pencil out of his drawer is $\frac{2}{3}$. There are 40 pencils; $\frac{40}{60} = \frac{4}{6} = \frac{2}{3}$.

b. The chance that Benjamin will take a red item out of his drawer is $\frac{1}{6}$. There are 10 red items in the drawer, so 10 out of 60 is $\frac{10}{60} = \frac{1}{6}$.

c. No. The chance that Benjamin will choose a red pencil is 8 out of 40, which is $\frac{1}{5}$.

Section C. Reasoning from Samples

1. **a.** The chance that a car is driving faster than 30 mi/h is about 15 out 63, which is 0.238, or about 24%.

b. $1 - 0.24 = 0.76$, or $100\% - 24\% = 76\%$.

Additional Practice

2. The table contains the results of a survey on the number of hours a day that students in middle school play video games. Jorge wants to know the chance that a student randomly chosen from this group that was surveyed plays video games for two or more hours a day.

Girls Hours per Day	1	1.5	2	0	0	1	1.5	3	3.5	1.5	1	2	1	2.5	1	1.5	1	0		
Boys Hours per Day	1	1	2	2	2.5	1.5	3	3	4	3.5	4	4.5	4	6	3.5	3	0	0	4	3.5

a. Organize the data in a two-way table like the one below and use the table to answer Jorge's question.

	Played Less Than 2 Hours Per Day	Played 2 or More Hours Per Day	Total
Boys			
Girls			
Total			

b. If a middle school student is chosen at random from this group, what is the chance that it is a girl who plays less than two hours of video games per day?

c. If you decide to choose a boy at random from the group, what is the chance he will play less than 2 hours of video games per day?

d. Jorge announced that the survey showed the chance that a seventh grader played two or more than two hours a day was about 53%. What do you think of his statement?

Section C. Reasoning from Sample (Continued)

2. a.

	Played Less than 2 Hours per Day	Played 2 or More Hours per Day	Total
Boys	5	15	20
Girls	13	5	18
Total	18	20	38

The chance of playing 2 or more hours per day is 20 out of 38, or about 53%.

b. The chance is 13 out of 38, or about 34%.

c. The chance is 5 out of 20, or 25%. This answer is different than the answer for part **b**. In part **b** you are picking from the whole group, so you have to compare the favorable outcome to the whole group. In part **c**, however, you are picking only from the boys, so you only have to compare the favorable outcome to the total number of boys.

d. Answers may vary. Sample answer:

The survey did not tell which grade the students were in, so Jorge could not really know anything about seventh graders from the results. The survey gave results for middle school students as a group; for students from this sample, 53% is correct.

One class did a survey and asked students what job they would like.

Students Future Jobs

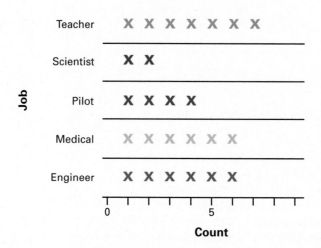

3. Can they conclude that being a teacher is the favorite choice for a career among students at their school?

Section **D** Expectations

A new dairy bar has opened on Baker Street. It serves only low-fat milk and yogurt drinks. The milk drinks cost $1.00, and the yogurt drinks cost $3.00. The owner does not yet know if his business will be successful. On his first day, 100 people place orders at the bar, 80% of whom order low-fat milk.

1. How much money did the dairy bar make on the first day of business? Draw a tree diagram to help you answer the problem.

The owner thinks that he may have overpriced the yogurt drink because most people are buying milk drinks. The second week, he reduces the price of his yogurt drinks to $2.50, but he does not want to lose money, so he raises the price of milk drinks to $1.50. He now expects to sell only 70% milk drinks and the rest yogurt drinks.

2. **a.** How much money does the owner expect to make if 100 people come to the dairy bar? Use a tree diagram to help you answer the problem.

   b. Has he lost income compared to his opening day?

Section C. Reasoning from Samples (Continued)

3. No, this is just a small sample, and the differences between the votes for teacher, a medical job, or engineer are very small.

Section D. Expectations

1. $80 + $60 = $140

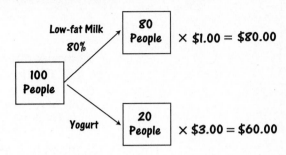

2. **a.** $105 + $75 = $180

   b. He has not lost income. He has gained $40.

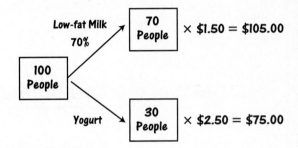

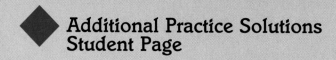
 Additional Practice

The owner changes the prices so that the milk and yogurt drinks each cost $2.00. He now expects to sell 40% yogurt drinks.

3. How much money does he expect to make with 100 customers? How does this compare to his previous income?

On the third week, the shop begins selling bagels for $1.00. It turns out that of the customers who buy milk drinks, 60% also buy a bagel. For customers who buy yogurt drinks, only 50% also buy a bagel.

4. How much money does the owner expect to make now if he has 100 customers?

Section E Combining Situations

Monica buys a ticket for the movies. Of the 240 seats in the theater, 80 are in the balcony.

Each seat in the theater has a number. The number of odd seats is the same as the number of even seats.

1. What is the chance that Monica will sit in the balcony?

2. a. What is the chance that Monica will sit in a seat with an even number that is not in the balcony?

   b. Explain whether or not you can use the multiplication rule for chance to answer **a**.

Section D. Expectations (Continued)

3. $200. Since all drinks cost $2.00, he expects to make $100 \times \$2.00 = \$200$. He has now earned another $20.

4. $256. One hundred milk or yogurt drinks at $2.00 each plus 56 bagels at $1.00 each equals $256.

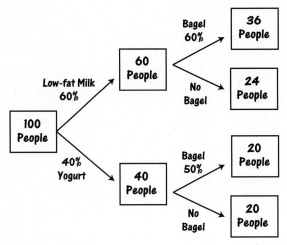

Section E. Combining Situations

1. 80 of the 240 seats are in the balcony, so the chance is $\frac{80}{240}$, or $\frac{1}{3}$.

2. a. Strategies will vary. Sample strategy:

Two-thirds of the seats are not in the balcony, and half of these seats have even numbers, so the probability is $\frac{2}{3} \times \frac{1}{2} = \frac{2}{6} = \frac{1}{3}$.

b. Yes, you can use the multiplication rule because of the two events. Having an odd number on the seat and a seat in the balcony are independent events.

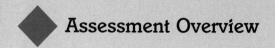

Assessment Overview

Unit assessments in *Mathematics in Context* include two quizzes and a Unit Test. Quiz 1 is to be used anytime after students have completed Section B. Quiz 2 can be used after students have completed Section D. The Unit Test addresses most of the major goals of the unit. You can evaluate student responses to these assessments to determine what each student knows about the content goals addressed in this unit.

Pacing

Each quiz is designed to take approximately 25 minutes to complete. The unit test is designed to be completed during a 45-minute class period. For more information on how to use these assessments, see the Planning Assessment section on the next page.

Goal	Assessment Opportunities	Problem Levels
• Use chance trees, counting strategies, two-way tables, and rules to find probability.	Quiz 1 Problem 2c Quiz 2 Problems 2ab Test Problems 3a, 4ac	Level I
• Use different representations (ratios, percents, fractions, and so on) to describe probability.	Quiz 2 Problems 2ab Test Problem 4a	
• Understand that variability is inherent in any probability situation.	Quiz 1 Problem 2c Quiz 2 Problem 2c	
• Use graphs and measures of central tendency to describe data.	Quiz 2 Problems 1ab	
• Reason about likely and unlikely samples and factors that can bias a survey.	Quiz 1 Problems 1ab, 2a Quiz 2 Problems 1c Test Problem 2	Level II
• Make decisions using probability and expected values.	Quiz 1 Problem 2c Quiz 2 Problem 2d Test Problems 4bc	
• Determine whether events are dependent or independent, and find the probabilities.	Quiz 1 Problem 2b Test Problems 1, 3b	

About the Mathematics

These assessment activities assess the majority of the goals for *Great Predictions*. Refer to the Goals and Assessment Opportunities section on the previous page for information regarding the goals that are assessed in each problem. Some of the problems that involve multiple skills and processes address more than one unit goal. To assess students' ability to make mathematical connections (a Level II goal in the Assessment Pyramid), some problems assess students' ability to choose an appropriate model or strategy to solve a problem.

For example, in the theater activity on the Unit Test (problem 4), students must apply their knowledge of probability models to make probabilistic decisions and determine expected values for a new problem context.

Planning Assessment

These assessments are designed for individual assessment; however, some problems can be done in pairs or small groups. It is important that students work individually if you want to evaluate each student's understanding and abilities.

Make sure you allow enough time for students to complete the problems. If students need more than one class session to complete the problems, it is suggested that they finish during the next mathematics class or you may assign select problems as a take-home activity. Students should be free to solve the problems their own way. Student use of calculators on these assessments is at the teachers' discretion.

If individual students have difficulties with any particular problems, you may give the student the option of making a second attempt after providing him or her a hint. You may also decide to use one of the optional problems or Extension activities not previously done in class as additional assessments for students who need additional help.

Scoring

Solution and scoring guides are included for each quiz and the Unit Test. The method of scoring depends on the types of questions on each assessment. A holistic scoring approach could also be used to evaluate an entire quiz.

Several problems require students to explain their reasoning or justify their answers. For these questions, the reasoning used by students in solving the problems, as well as the correctness of the answers, should be considered in your scoring and grading scheme.

Student progress toward goals of the unit should be considered when reviewing student work. Descriptive statements and specific feedback are often more informative to students than a total score or grade. You might choose to record descriptive statements of select aspects of student work as evidence of student progress toward specific goals of the unit that you have identified as essential.

Use additional paper as needed.

1. Mary wants to know whether students at her school, Julian Middle School, prefer to go to the movies or prefer to watch TV. She interviewed 12 of her friends, and based on their preferences, she decided that $\frac{1}{4}$ of the school prefers to go to the movies and $\frac{3}{4}$ prefers to watch TV.

   a. Do you think Mary's results are reliable? Explain why or why not.

   b. Julian Middle School has a total of 324 students. Describe another way to find out whether students at Julian Middle School prefer going to the movies or stay home to watch TV. Make sure your method will provide reliable results.

2. At Julian Middle School a random sample of all students completed a survey that asked questions about how many hours a week they spend doing homework. The results of the survey are shown in the table below.

	Less Than 3 Hours a Week	3 or More Hours a Week	Total
Girls	38	31	**69**
Boys	50	31	**81**
Total	**88**	**62**	**150**

   a. Explain what is meant by a "random sample of all students" in this situation.

b. Tora states: "There is no connection between hours spent on school work at home and being a boy or girl, since the same number of boys (31) and girls (31) spend 3 or more hours a week on homework." Do you agree with Tora? Why or why not? Support your answer mathematically.

c. Below are four statements about this survey. For each statement, indicate whether the statement is a **good** conclusion that can be drawn from the survey or a **poor** conclusion. Explain your ratings for each statement.

i. Girls at Julian Middle School work harder than boys.

ii. I expect that about 60% of all boys at Julian Middle School spend less than 3 hours a week doing homework.

iii. If you randomly choose a student from the group of 150, it is more likely that it will be a boy than a girl.

iv. If you randomly choose a student from the group of 150, it is more likely that this student spends three or more hours doing homework (instead of less than three hours).

Great Predictions Quiz 2

Use additional paper as needed.

1. Mary complains that the school bus often arrives late.
For 31 days, she recorded how many minutes the bus was
delayed. If the bus arrived on time or early, she recorded
zero minutes. She made a histogram of the data:

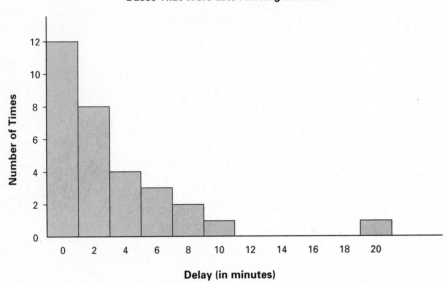

Buses That Were Late Arriving at School

Mary considers the bus late if it is delayed two or more minutes.

a. Suppose you select at random one of the 31 days she recorded
this information. What is the chance that on this day the bus
will be between 2 and 4 minutes late? Show your work.

b. Based on the information in this graph, what conclusion
should Mary make? Show your work.

c. Assume you are the owner of the bus company. What aspects
of Mary's survey methods would you criticize?

Mathematics in Context

2. John is playing a computer game where he has to shoot a
ball at a goal. If he misses on the first try, he can shoot a
second time. John says he misses about 40% of the time on
his first try and 30% of the time on his second try.

a. John plays the game once. What is the chance that John
misses the goal both times? Make a chance tree that shows
the possible outcomes.

b. What is the chance that John misses on his first try and
hits the goal on his second try?

c. John plays the game 10 times. Is it possible for him to hit
the goal 8 out of 10 times on his first try?

d. John plays the game 100 times and gets 1 point for each
goal he scores. What is his average expected score of
points per game?

Great Predictions Unit Test

Use additional paper as needed.

1. On Swanson's car lot, one-half of the cars in stock have
antilock brakes. Ten percent of the cars in stock are red.
Every morning, the dealer randomly chooses a different
car to put in the showroom window. There is no connection
between a car's being red and having antilock brakes.

What is the chance that the car in the showroom window
on a particular day has antilock brakes and is red? Write an
explanation describing how you calculated the chance.
You may want to use a diagram to illustrate your explanation.

2. The following announcement was in a newspaper.

Herald Phone Poll[*]

This week's question:

Should the city arrest people who open fire hydrants in the summer?

Vote YES dial 257-YYES

Vote NO dial 257-NNNO

[*] The Herald Poll is not scientifically designed; therefore, no claims are made as to its accuracy.

Explain why the people running the poll included the statement at the bottom of the announcement.

Great Predictions Unit Test

Use additional paper as needed.

3. Mr. Smith works in the school administration of Bora Middle School. He wants to find out how students come to school, either by car or by school bus (nobody walks or rides a bike to school). One day, he took a survey of a sample of students in two grades. He organized the results into the following table:

Transport	Car	Bus	Total
Grade 5	11	17	28
Grade 6	5	21	26
Total	16	38	

a. Based on these results, would you expect that coming to school by car depends upon the grade level of the student? Show your work.

b. Mr. Smith repeated the survey with another group students from the same grade levels. The results were organized into the following table.

Transport	Car	Bus	Total
Grade 5	66	245	
Grade 6	52	223	
Total			

Based on the results of the larger sample, would you come to a different conclusion than the one you gave for Problem 4a about the connection between coming to school by car and grade? Support your answer with an explanation or by showing your work.

Mathematics in Context

4. A theater recorded the number of tickets that were sold at a reduced price of $9. For most shows, the percent of tickets sold at the reduced price is about 40%. For next week's show, the manager wants to estimate the total amount of ticket sales. The price of a regular ticket is $12.

a. The manager expects 200 tickets to be sold for next week's show. What amount of money should the theater owner expect to make next week on ticket sales?

b. What could happen to the total amount if the manager decides to make the reduced tickets a little cheaper? Give an example and give reasons to support your answer.

c. Peter wants to see the show, but all of the tickets are sold out. He expects that about 2% of the people who bought a ticket for that day will decide to skip the show. Peter also expects that one fifth of the people who skip the show will try to sell their ticket to someone else at the theater before the show begins. The theater holds about 500 people.

What is the chance that Peter will be able to purchase a ticket if he goes to the theater right before the show begins? Show your work.

Possible student answer	Suggested number of score points	Problem level
1. a. Mary's results are probably NOT reliable. Sample explanation: Mary only asked her friends, and these may not represent the preferences of most students.	**2**	**II**
b. Different answers are possible. Sample answer: • Mary could randomly choose 10 students from each class or grade level and interview them.	**2** (Award 1 point for an alternative method and 1 point for a correct explanation.)	**II**
2. a. Sample answer: Each student at Julian Middle School has an equal chance of being in the sample.	**1**	**II**
b. Sample answer: I do not agree with Tora. • 31 out of 69 girls (or about 45%) spend 3 hours a week or more on their homework; 31 out of 81 boys (or about 38%) spend 3 hours a week or more on their homework. • 38 out of 69 girls (or about 55%) spend less than 3 hours a week doing homework, whereas 50 out of 81 boys (or about 62%) do so.	**3** (Award 1 point for a correct conclusion and, 2 points for correct computation.)	**II**
c. i. Poor conclusion. A higher percentage of girls spend more hours on homework, but the difference between girls and boys seems relatively small. **ii.** Good conclusion. The sample was random, so you may expect the ratio of boys and girls to be the same for the whole school as in this sample. **iii.** Good conclusion. There are more boys than girls in the sample. **iv.** Poor conclusion. 88 out of 150 students spend less than 3 hours doing homework, and 62 out of 150 spend more than 3 hours. It is more likely a randomly chosen student belongs to the first group of 88 because this group is larger .	**4** (Award 1 point for each correct answer.)	**I/II**
Total score points	**12**	

Possible student answer	Suggested number of score points	Problem level
1. a. The chance is 8 out of 31, or about 25%.	**2**	**I**
b. Mary will conclude that the bus is usually late. Sample calculations: • In 31 days, the bus is late 2 minutes or more 19 times. Therefore, the bus is delayed about 61% of the time. • The bus arrives on time 12 days out of 31. The bus is on time about 39% of the time.	**2** (1 point for a correct conclusion based on the data and, 1 point for correct calculations.)	**I**
c. Sample answers: (Note: Students only need to give one reason.) • This was a small sample. You cannot draw these conclusions if you only observe what happens over one month. • Her sample was not randomly selected. In this time of the year, traffic is always bad because of weather conditions, and the safety of the children is our top priority! She should have measured, for example, several times a week over many months. • Perhaps in this month, there were more traffic jams than usual. • The bus driver is a new driver without much experience. Give him time to get used to the route.	**2**	**II**
2. a. The chance is about 12%. Sample explanations: • I started with 100 first tries and found that 12 out of 100 times both shots failed to hit the goal. • The chance both shots failed is $\frac{40}{100} \times \frac{30}{100} = \frac{12}{100} = 12\%$. 40% of 30% is 12%.	**3** (Award 2 points for a correct chance tree and 1 point for a correct answer.)	**I**

Possible student answer	Suggested number of score points	Problem level
b. The chance is 28%. $\frac{40}{100} \times \frac{70}{100} = \frac{4}{10} \times \frac{7}{10} = \frac{28}{100}$.	**2**	**I**
c. Yes, this is possible. You would expect John to hit the goal 60% of the time on his first try. So 8 out of 10 seems quite possible. It is actually possible for John to hit 10 in a row, although it is not likely.	**2** (Award 1 point for "yes" and 1 point for a correct explanation.)	**I**
d. He has an expected score of 88 points for the 100 games, which is an average expected score per game of 0.88 points. For 100 games, he scores 60 on his first try and 28 on his second try. So he scores 88 points in all over 100 games.	**2** (Award 1 point for the answer, one for the calculation.)	**II**
Total score points	**15**	

Possible student answer	Suggested number of score points	Problem level
1. 0.05, or 5%. Sample strategies: Strategy 1: Students might multiply the two individual chances: $0.5 \times 0.1 = 0.05$ or 5% (or 50% × 10% = 5%). Strategy 2: Students might use a chance tree. I assumed there were 300 cars on the lot. Half of the cars (150) had antilock brakes. One-tenth of the 150 cars were red ($\frac{1}{10} \times 150 = 15$ cars). So, the chance that a car is red and has antilock brakes is $\frac{15}{300}$, which is 0.05 or 5%.	2	II
2. Sample response: The poll results may be biased due to the sampling method used. The poll is not scientifically designed since the survey responses are only from people who phone in, not from a randomly selected sample. People who have strong feelings one-way or the other are the ones who will respond. People who do not respond may have an opinion, but they may not feel strongly enough about it to call in. In addition, the survey will only reach those who read the newspaper that day, which is not a random group of people.	2	II

Possible student answer	Suggested number of score points	Problem level
3. a. 	Car	Bus	Total
---	---	---	---
Grade 5	11 (39%)	17	28
Grade 6	5 (19%)	21	26
Total	16 (30%)	38	54 | Yes this seems dependent. Of the Grade 5 students, 11 out of 28 (or 39%) took a car to school. Of the Grade 6 students, 5 out of 26 (or 19%) took a car to school. This difference is rather large.	2	I
b. Yes, the larger sample leads to a different conclusion from the small sample. Now the percentages for students in the two grades coming to school by car are almost the same. So coming by car does seem to be independent of the grade level.	2	II

Table for 3.a:

Transport	Car	Bus	Total
Grade 5	11 (39%)	17	28
Grade 6	5 (19%)	21	26
Total	16 (30%)	38	54

Table for 3.b:

Transport	Car	Bus	Total
Grade 5	66 (21%)	245	311
Grade 6	52 (19%)	223	275
Total	118 (20%)	468	586

4. a. The expected amount is $2,160.

Sample work:

40% of 200 is 80 tickets, and 80 × $9 = $720.

So $720 is the income for the **reduced tickets.**

120 × $12 = $1,440 is the income for the **regular tickets.**

In total: $720 + $1,440 = $2,160.

Suggested number of score points: 2 — Problem level: I

b. Sample answers:
- If the same number of people come to the show, the total amount of money will be lower, because the price of the reduced tickets is lower.

  80 tickets × $8 = $640
  120 tickets × $12 = $1,440
              $2,080

Suggested number of score points: 2 — Problem level: II

Possible student answer	Suggested number of score points	Problem level
• More people may be expected to come because the reduced tickets are cheaper. In that case, it is possible that the total amount will be equal or even higher. 100 tickets × \$8 = \$800 120 tickets × \$12 = \$1,440 ——————————————— $2,240 **c.** Different strategies may be used. Sample answer using a chance tree: The chance of Peter finding tickets to the show is $\frac{2}{100} \times \frac{1}{5} = \frac{1}{250}$, which is 0.004, or 0.4%. So 0.4% × 500 tickets = 2 tickets.	2	I/II
Total score points	14	

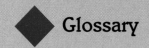 Glossary

Glossary

The Glossary defines all vocabulary words indicated in this unit. It includes the mathematical terms that may be new to students, as well as words having to do with the contexts introduced in the unit. (Note: The Student Book has no glossary. Instead, students are encouraged to construct their own definitions, based on their personal experiences with the unit activities.)

The definitions below are specific for the use of the terms in this unit. The page numbers given are from the Student Book.

bias (TG p. 1T) an inclination to choose a sample that is not representative of the whole, which would favor certain outcomes and provide untrue data

chance (TG p. 2T) the likelihood of an event's occurring; the number of times an event occurs divided by the total number of all possible occurrences

chance tree (p. 19) a pictorial representation of a probability situation in which all outcomes are shown and their probabilities given

complement (p. 30) two independent events for a given situation that, when combined together, represent all the outcomes (with a combined probability of 100%)

dependent events (p. 15) events for which the outcomes are connected

expected value (p. 34) the amount or number that is expected; this can be a total or a rate

independent events (p. 15) events for which the outcomes are not connected

multiplication rule for chance (p. 44) the chance for a combination of events to occur; the chance of the first event to occur times the chance of the second event to occur

population (p. 4) any group of individuals

probability (p. 5) the chance or likelihood of an event's occurrence; the number of favorable outcomes divided by the total number of possible outcomes

sample (p. 4) a group taken from a larger population

simulation (TG p. 24T) a model of a chance situation often used to gather experimental data

tree diagram (TG p. 14T) a diagram with branches representing all possible choices or combinations of choices

uncertainty (TG p. 1B) something about which you cannot make a determination

BRITANNICA

Mathematics
in
Context

Blackline
Masters

Dear Family,

Your child is starting the *Mathematics in Context* unit *Great Predictions*. Below is a letter to your child that introduces the unit and its goals.

Surveys are used extensively in politics and business. In this unit, your child will have the opportunity to investigate how probability and statistics can be used to evaluate survey results.

You can help your child to relate classwork to his or her own life by finding the results of a survey in a newspaper or magazine and discussing the data. Discuss why the survey was taken and what might be done with the results. Look for important information, such as who sponsored the survey, how the respondents were selected, and what questions they were asked.

You might discuss ways in which chance and probability play important roles in everyday life—in forecasting the weather, in predicting the likelihood that a certain sports team will win the big game or that a local politician will win a senate race, and so on.

We have great expectations that you and your child will enjoy investigating probability and statistics.

Sincerely,

The Mathematics in Context Development Team

Dear Student,

Welcome to Great Predictions!

Surveys report that teens prefer brand-name jeans over any other jeans.

Do you think you can believe all the conclusions that are reported as "survey results"? How can the results be true if they are based on the responses of just a few people?

In this unit, you will investigate how statistics can help you study, and answer, those questions. As you explore the activities in this unit, watch for articles in newspapers and magazines about surveys. Bring them to class and discuss how the ideas of this unit help you interpret the surveys.

When you finish *Great Predictions*, you will appreciate how people use statistics to interpret surveys and make decisions.

Sincerely,

The Mathematics in Context Development Team

◆ **Student Activity Sheet 2**
Use with *Great Predictions*,
pages 24 and 25.

Name_____

GE Fish Lengths

28
26
24
22
20
18
16
14
12
10
8

Length (in cm)

Original Fish Lengths

28
26
24
22
20
18
16
14
12
10
8

Length (in cm)

Name _____

Student Activity Sheet 3 ◆
Use with *Great Predictions*,
pages 26 and 27.

Length of GE Fish

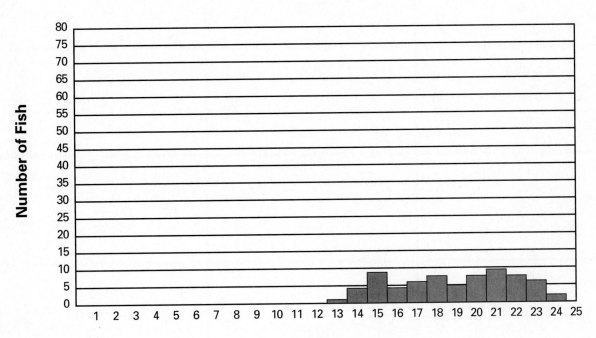

Length of Original Fish

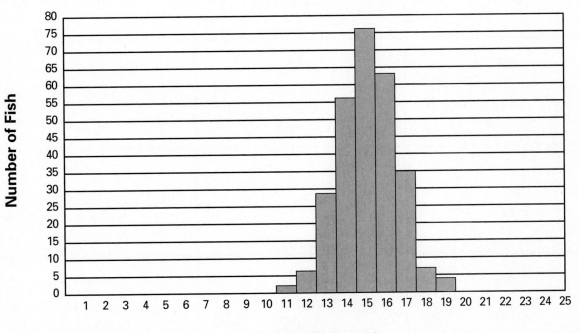

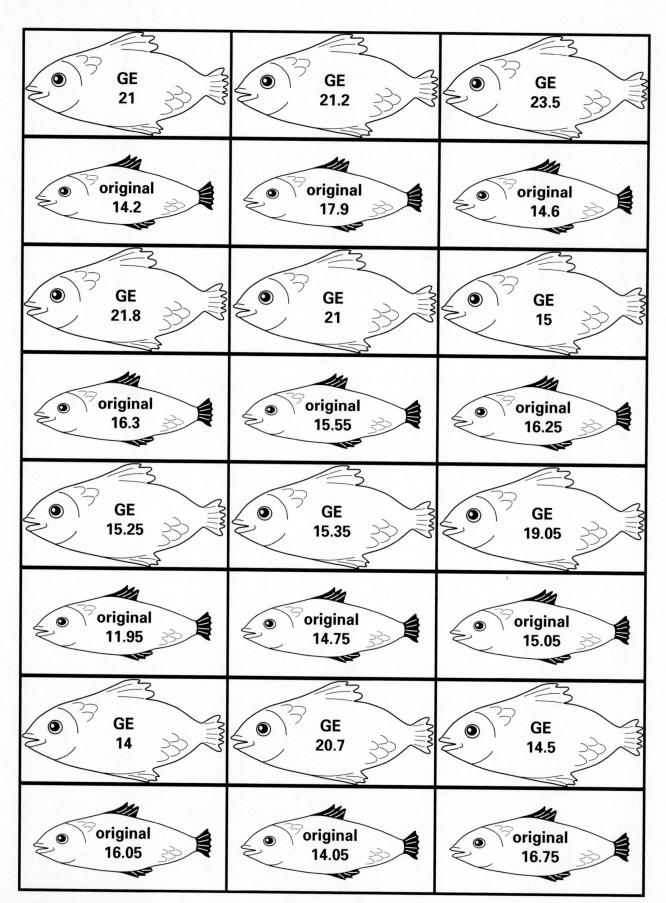

GE
21

GE
21.2

GE
23.5

original
14.2

original
17.9

original
14.6

GE
21.8

GE
21

GE
15

original
16.3

original
15.55

original
16.25

GE
15.25

GE
15.35

GE
19.05

original
11.95

original
14.75

original
15.05

GE
14

GE
20.7

GE
14.5

original
16.05

original
14.05

original
16.75

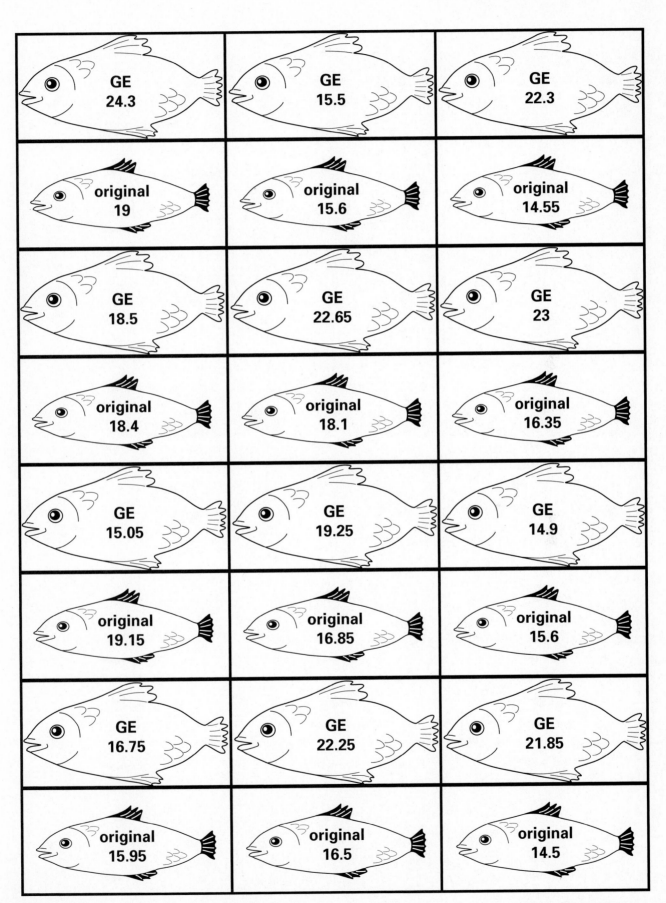

GE
24.3

GE
15.5

GE
22.3

original
19

original
15.6

original
14.55

GE
18.5

GE
22.65

GE
23

original
18.4

original
18.1

original
16.35

GE
15.05

GE
19.25

GE
14.9

original
19.15

original
16.85

original
15.6

GE
16.75

GE
22.25

GE
21.85

original
15.95

original
16.5

original
14.5

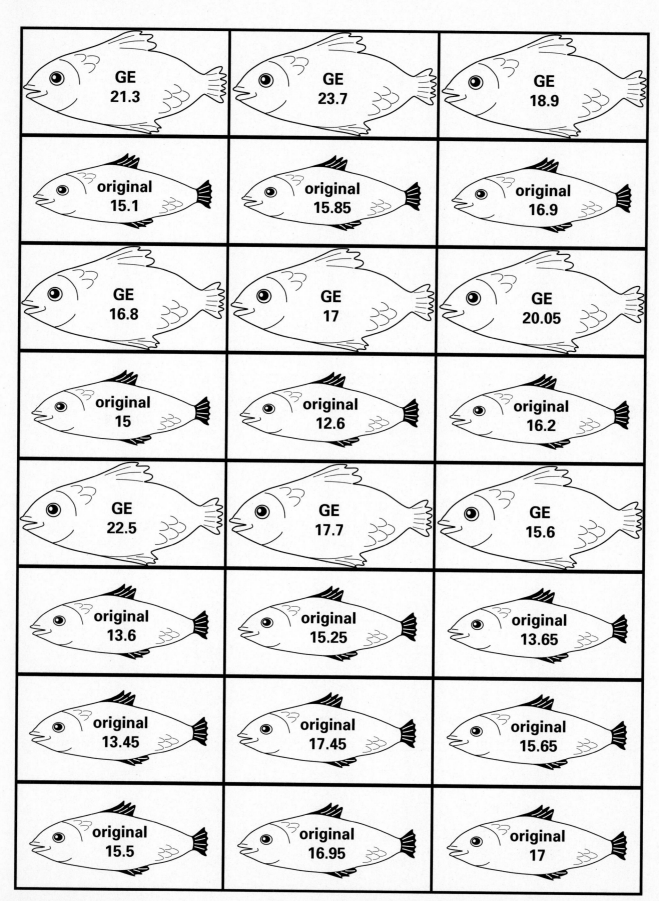

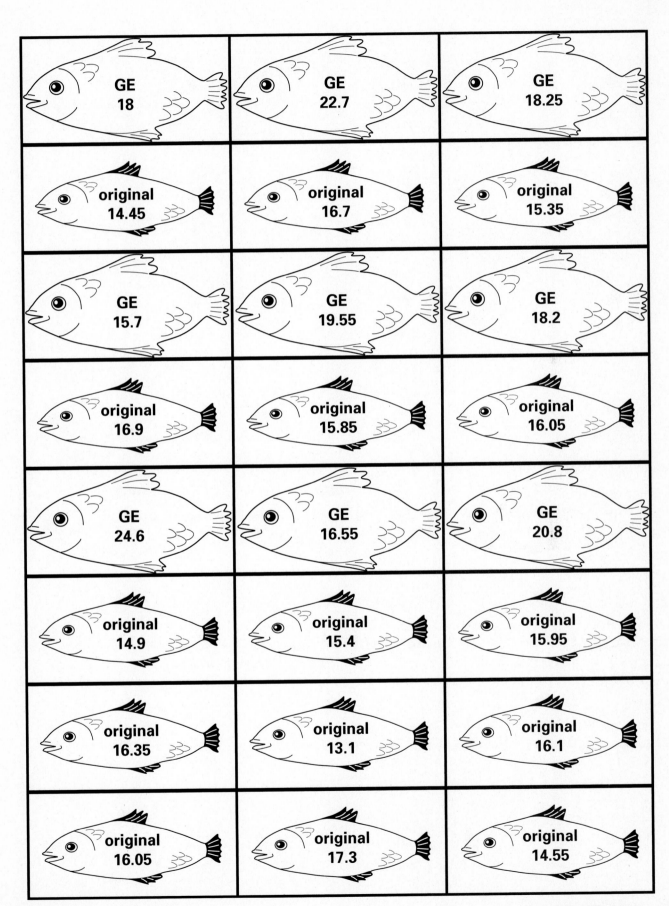

GE
18

GE
22.7

GE
18.25

original
14.45

original
16.7

original
15.35

GE
15.7

GE
19.55

GE
18.2

original
16.9

original
15.85

original
16.05

GE
24.6

GE
16.55

GE
20.8

original
14.9

original
15.4

original
15.95

original
16.35

original
13.1

original
16.1

original
16.05

original
17.3

original
14.55

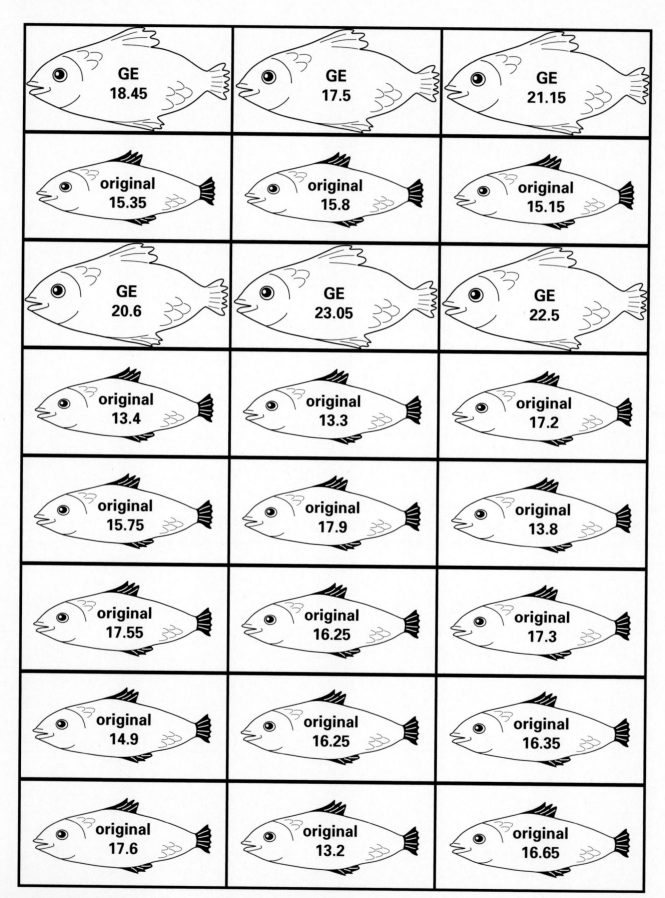

GE
18.45

GE
17.5

GE
21.15

original
15.35

original
15.8

original
15.15

GE
20.6

GE
23.05

GE
22.5

original
13.4

original
13.3

original
17.2

original
15.75

original
17.9

original
13.8

original
17.55

original
16.25

original
17.3

original
14.9

original
16.25

original
16.35

original
17.6

original
13.2

original
16.65

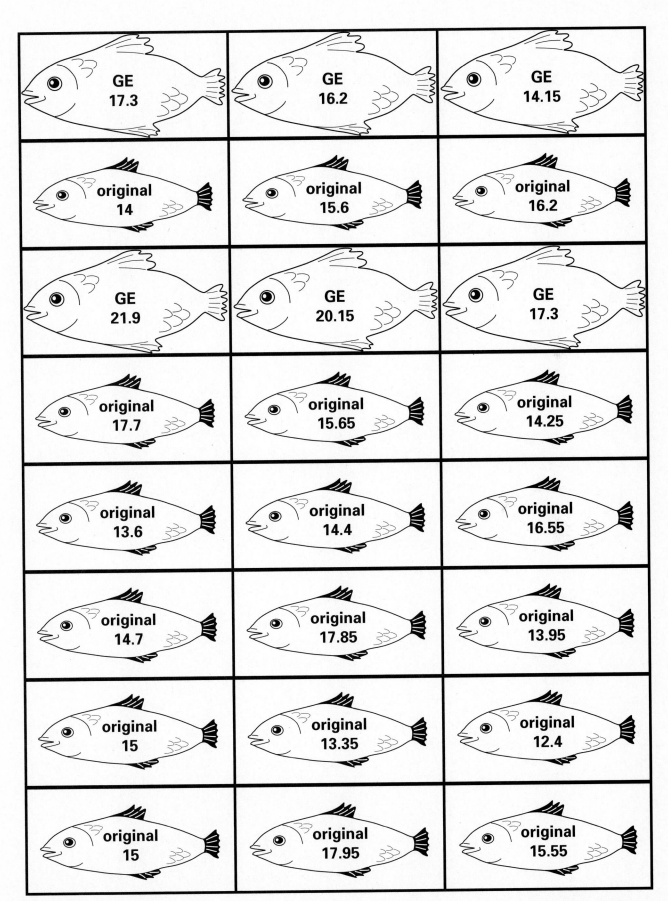

GE
17.3

GE
16.2

GE
14.15

original
14

original
15.6

original
16.2

GE
21.9

GE
20.15

GE
17.3

original
17.7

original
15.65

original
14.25

original
13.6

original
14.4

original
16.55

original
14.7

original
17.85

original
13.95

original
15

original
13.35

original
12.4

original
15

original
17.95

original
15.55

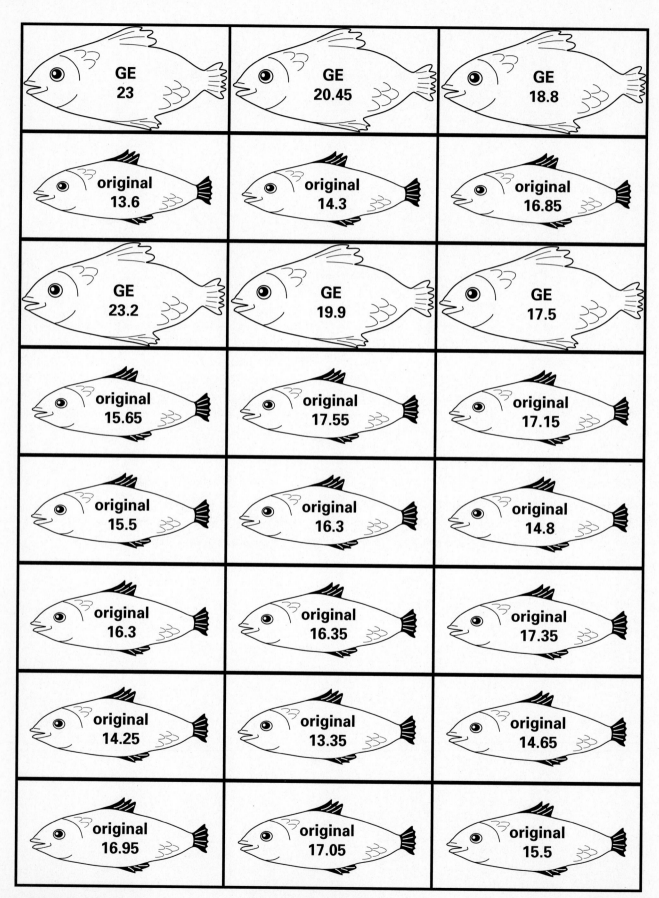

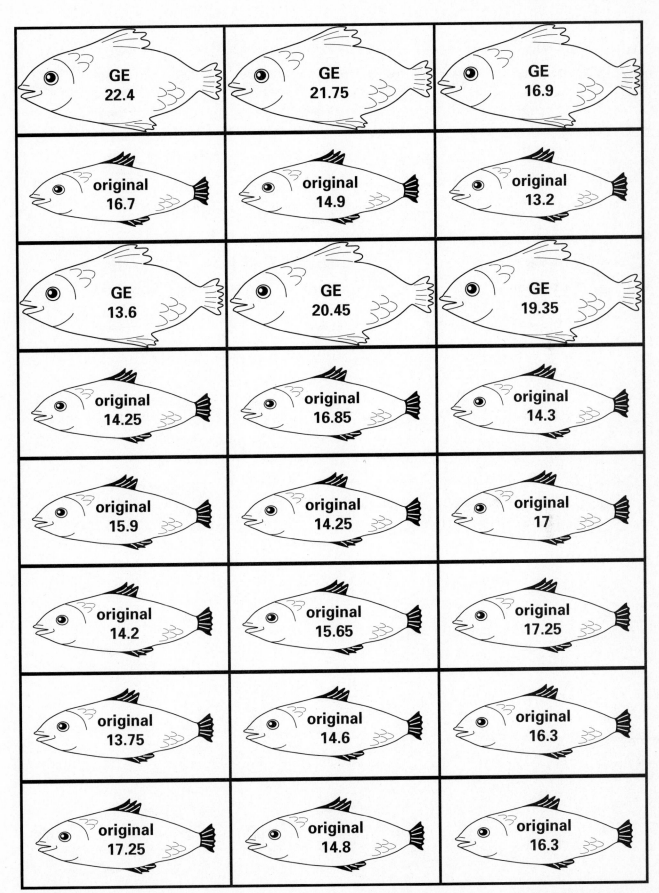

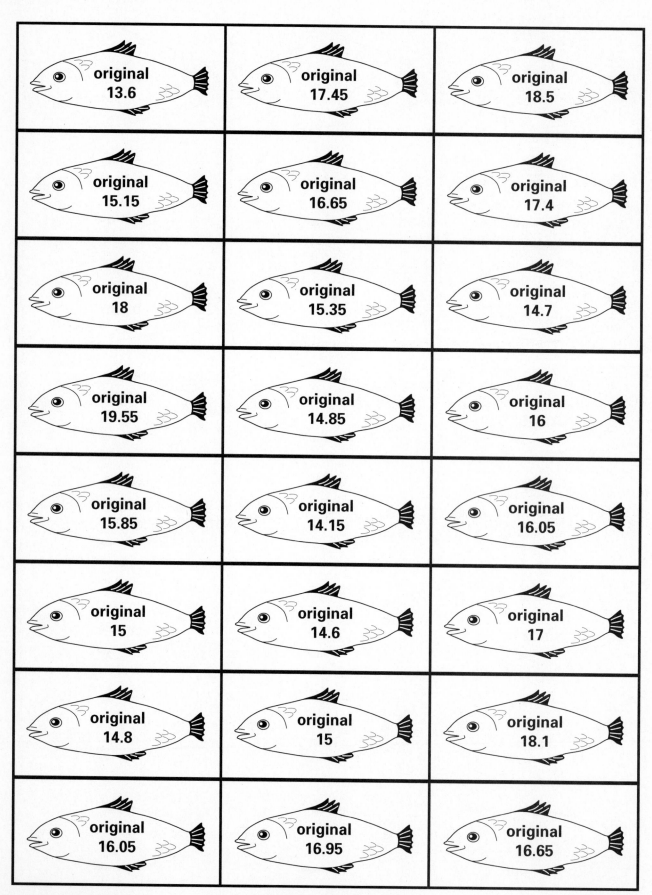

original 13.6	original 17.45	original 18.5
original 15.15	original 16.65	original 17.4
original 18	original 15.35	original 14.7
original 19.55	original 14.85	original 16
original 15.85	original 14.15	original 16.05
original 15	original 14.6	original 17
original 14.8	original 15	original 18.1
original 16.05	original 16.95	original 16.65

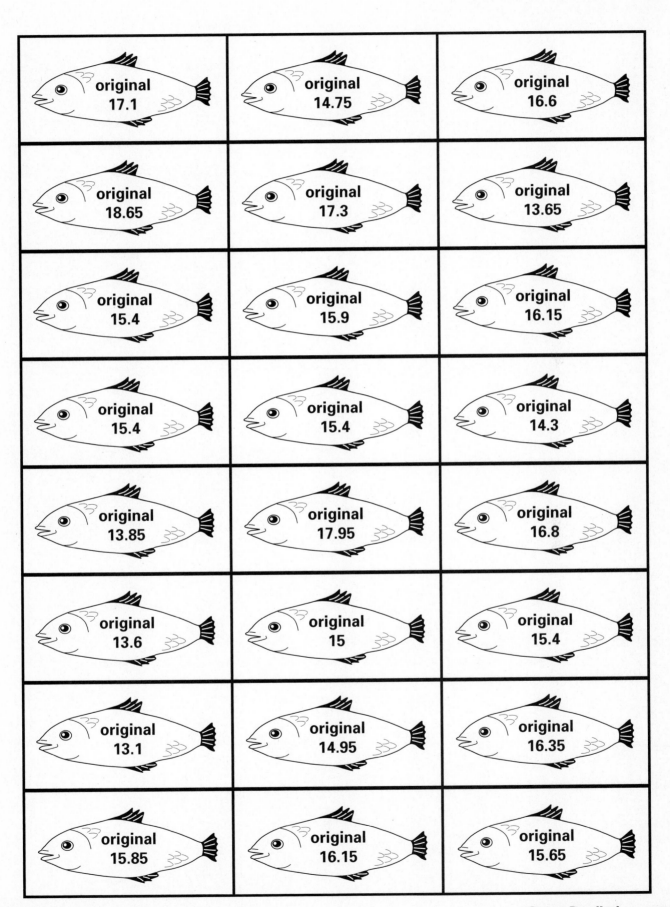

original
17.1

original
14.75

original
16.6

original
18.65

original
17.3

original
13.65

original
15.4

original
15.9

original
16.15

original
15.4

original
15.4

original
14.3

original
13.85

original
17.95

original
16.8

original
13.6

original
15

original
15.4

original
13.1

original
14.95

original
16.35

original
15.85

original
16.15

original
15.65

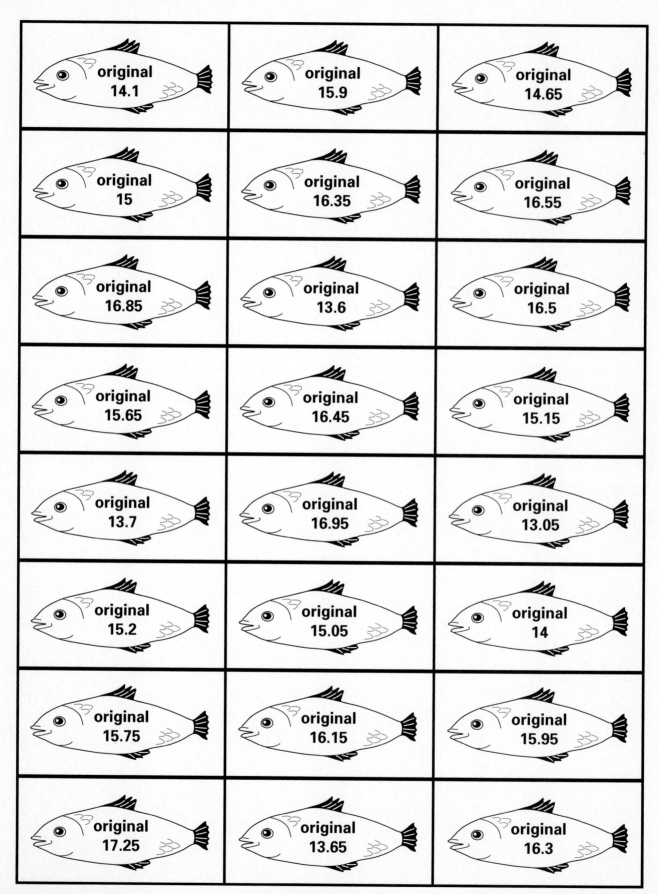

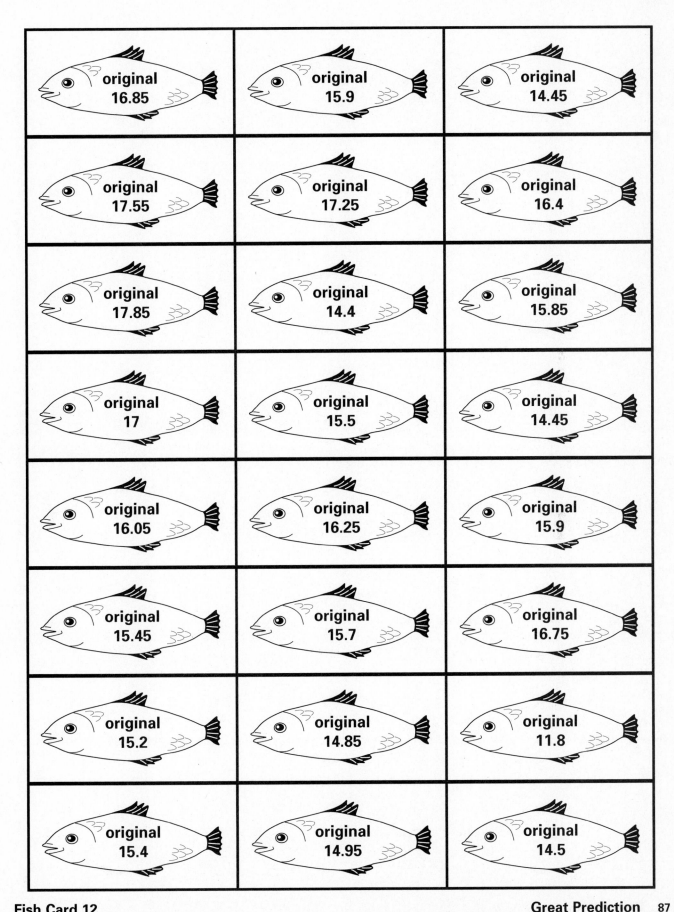

original 16.85	original 15.9	original 14.45
original 17.55	original 17.25	original 16.4
original 17.85	original 14.4	original 15.85
original 17	original 15.5	original 14.45
original 16.05	original 16.25	original 15.9
original 15.45	original 15.7	original 16.75
original 15.2	original 14.85	original 11.8
original 15.4	original 14.95	original 14.5

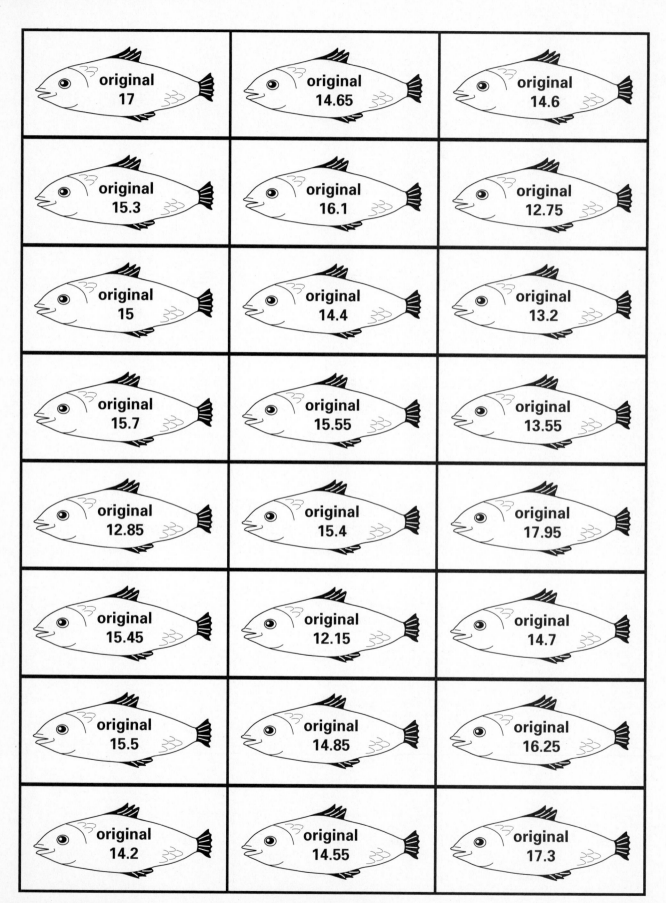

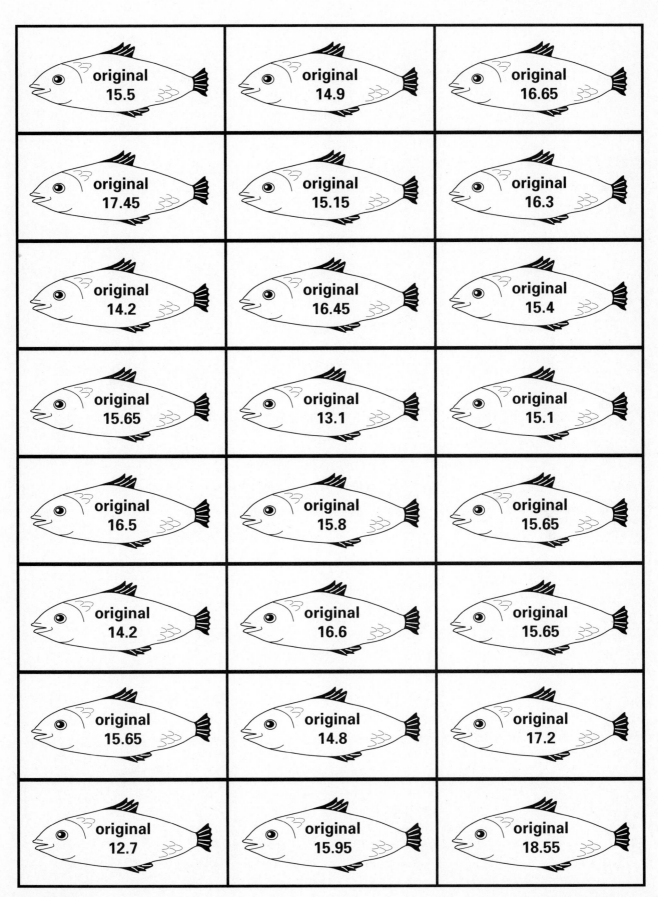

original
15.5

original
14.9

original
16.65

original
17.45

original
15.15

original
16.3

original
14.2

original
16.45

original
15.4

original
15.65

original
13.1

original
15.1

original
16.5

original
15.8

original
15.65

original
14.2

original
16.6

original
15.65

original
15.65

original
14.8

original
17.2

original
12.7

original
15.95

original
18.55

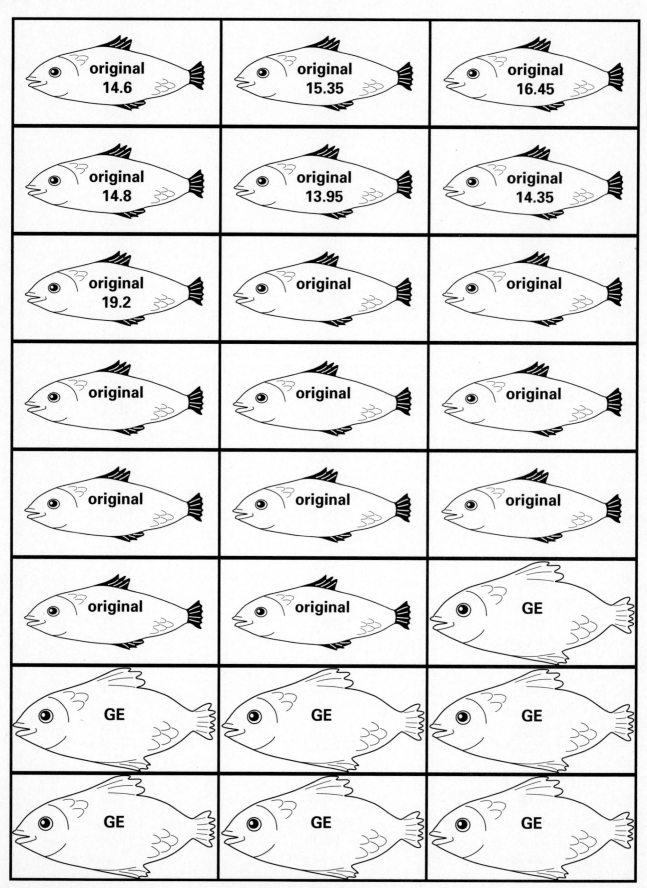

5. **Reflect** If something unusual happened in your life, how would you decide whether it was due to chance or something else? Give an example.

Taking Samples

Here are some terms that are helpful when you want to talk about chance.

A **population** is the whole group in which you are interested.

A **sample** is a part of that population.

In a town of 400 people, 80 subscribe to the local newspaper. This could be represented in a diagram in which 80 out of 400 squares have been filled in randomly. So the red squares represent the subscribers.

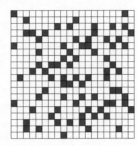

A researcher wants to take a random sample of ten people from the population in the town. You are going to simulate taking the sample by using the diagram on **Student Activity Sheet 1**.

Activity

Close your eyes and hold your pencil over the diagram on **Student Activity Sheet 1**. Let the tip of your pencil land lightly on the diagram. Open your eyes and note where the tip landed.

Do this experiment a total of 10 times, keeping track of how many times you land on a black square. The 10 squares that you land on are a sample.

Hints and Comments
(continued from page 4T)

Extension or Alternative Using Technology

2. a. As a group, investigate sample sizes of 40, 60, and 100. For each different sample size, decide how many marked dots you would expect. Then record the actual number of marked dots for that sample. What observations can you make? (answers: number of expected marked dots are: 8, 12, and 20 respectively)

   b. Compare your results with those of other groups. What conclusions can you draw?

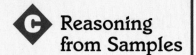

2. **a.** Write at least two observations about the lengths of the two types of fish based on the plots you made with your group. One observation should be about the mean length of the fish.

   b. Compare your observations with the observations of another group. What do you notice?

The fish farmer claimed that GE fish grew twice the size of the original fish.

3. Based on your data about the length of fish in the plots, do you agree or disagree with the fish farmer's claim about the length of the GE fish? Support your answer.

Add all the data points from every student in your class to the plots.

4. Now would you change your answer to problem 3?

5. What claim could you make about the lengths of the GE fish compared to the original fish based on the graphs of the whole class data? How would you justify your claim?

The fish farmer only wants to sell fish that are 17 centimeters (cm) or longer.

6. **a.** Based on the results of the simulation activity from your class, estimate the chance that a randomly caught GE fish is 17 cm or longer.

   b. Estimate the chance that a randomly caught original fish is 17 cm or longer.

   c. Estimate the chance that a randomly caught fish is 17 cm or longer. How did you arrive at your estimate?

Hints and Comments
(continued from page 25T)

Overview

Students combine the data from their samples into one big sample. They study this sample and draw conclusions about the lengths of the two types of fish.

About the Mathematics

By graphing data, the underlying distribution becomes visible. In this case, the data are the length of fish. The distribution of the lengths approaches the normal distribution (bell-shaped curve); as the sample size gets larger, the data in the sample will also approach the normal distribution. Students can characterize data with measures of center like mean or median, combined with the spread in data. This was addressed in the unit *Dealing with Data*.

Planning

Students may work on problems 2 and 3 in small groups. You may want to discuss their answers in class. Problem 4 is a whole-class activity; you could use either the overhead or draw a large graph on the board or flip chart. Problems 5–6 can be done individually or in pairs.

Comments About the Solutions

3. You may want to discuss how the data from their sample can influence the conclusions and how reliable students think their conclusions are.

4. Discuss the effect of the growing sample in class. Most likely the general pattern will not change much, but the distribution of lengths from the GE fish will become more clear.

5. Students may have different opinions but should have good reasons for their decisions. They may feel that the sample sizes are too small to make any good decision.

7. a. If you caught an original fish at random, what length (roughly) is most likely? Use the data in the histograms and give reasons for your answer.

   b. If you caught a GE fish, what length would be most likely?

Remember: The fish farmer only wants to sell fish that are 17 cm or longer.

8. a. Based on the information in these graphs, estimate the chance that a randomly caught original fish will be 17 cm or longer.

   b. Estimate the chance that a randomly caught GE fish will be 17 cm or longer.

   c. Estimate the chance of randomly catching a fish that is 17 cm or longer.

9. a. Compare your answers to problems 6 and 8. Are they similar? If they are very different, what might explain the difference?

   b. Why is the answer to 8c closer to the answer to 8a than to the answer for 8b?

You can use a two-way table to organize the lengths of the fish that were caught.

	Up to 17 cm	17 cm or Longer	Total
Original			
GE			
Total			343

10. a. Copy the two-way table into your notebook and fill in the correct numbers using the data from the histograms for the total of 343 fish. You already have a few of those numbers.

   b. What is the chance the fish farmer will catch a GE fish?

   c. **Reflect** How can you calculate in an easy way the chance that he will catch an original fish?

   d. What is the chance that he catches an original fish that is 17 cm or longer?

   e. Which type of fish do you advise the fish farmer to raise? Be sure to give good reasons for your advice.

Hints and Comments (continued from page 27T)

About the Mathematics

Data can be distributed in several ways. A very common distribution is the normal distribution that shows as a bell-shaped curve. The two histograms of the length of the fish that students study on this page are very different in shape: one has a kind of bell shape; the other one is flatter. Students must try to characterize the distribution in an overall sense instead of just by looking at individual data points. This is a very important ability in statistics and probability. They can talk about these shapes using informal terms like "bump," "flat," "spread out," and so on.

Students compare the two distributions and reason about the chances of catching fish of different lengths. The data from the two types of fish and their lengths can be combined into one two-way table to find out if a connection exists between length and type of fish.

Planning

Students can work on problems 7–10 individually or in pairs.

Comments About the Solutions

7. You may want to have students describe the differences in the shapes of the distributions of the lengths.

9. Whether the sample size will influence the statements about chance will depend on the samples students took. A larger sample does not necessarily give a different chance. Because the samples will vary, it is reasonable to expect some variation in the calculations. Students would need to be concerned if they found a sample that was very different from what they might expect based on the others.